BOEING 757

A Legends of Flight Illustrated History

DAN DORNSEIF

SCHIFFER MILITARY
4880 Lower Valley Road   Atglen, PA 19310

Designed by Justin Watkinson
Cover design by Molly Shields
Type set in DIN/Minion Pro

ISBN: 978-0-7643-6346-7
Printed in India

Published by Schiffer Publishing, Ltd.
4880 Lower Valley Road
Atglen, PA 19310
Phone: (610) 593-1777; Fax: (610) 593-2002
Email: Info@schifferbooks.com
Web: www.schifferbooks.com

For our complete selection of fine books on this and related subjects, please visit our website at www.schifferbooks.com. You may also write for a free catalog.

Schiffer Publishing's titles are available at special discounts for bulk purchases for sales promotions or premiums. Special editions, including personalized covers, corporate imprints, and excerpts, can be created in large quantities for special needs. For more information, contact the publisher.

We are always looking for people to write books on new and related subjects. If you have an idea for a book, please contact us at proposals@ schifferbooks.com.

CONTENTS

ACKNOWLEDGMENTS

This historical and technical look at the Boeing 757 would not have been possible without the generous cooperation from many people who were on the scene when the airplane was developed, designed, tested, and certified. Many spent countless hours helping to bring information together so that the true history can be shared with the public. Many topics are being explored for the first time, bringing the story of this magnificent aircraft to life. Most importantly, because of the support of the Boeing Company and the individuals listed below, the "people" side of the story is now being told. Thus, I owe each a debt of gratitude to them for their support and assistance: Gabrielle Adelman, Dave Anderson, D. Paul Angel, John Armstrong, Chuck Ballard, Paul Belshaw, Bob Bogash, Pat Boone, Murray Booth, Zac Christenson, Dr. Phil Condit, Barry Cooper, Don Cumming, Robert Davis, John Dulski, Delmar Fadden, Bruce Florsheim, Clifford Forester, Sandy Graham, Jennings Heilig, John Hindmarch, Thomas Imrich, Thomas Imrich Jr., Duane Jackson, Jim Johnson, Garth Jones, George Kanellis, Barry Latter, Rick Lentz, Michael Lombardi, Tom Lubbesmeyer, Avtar Mahal, Glen Marshall, Bill McIntosh, Fred Mitchell, Peter Morton, Ahmed Orgunwall, Peter Rinearson, Steven Sauck, Joe Sutter, Dick Taylor, Marlene Taylor-Houtchens, Steve Taylor, Larry Timmons, Max Welliver, Jack Wimpress, and Flip Wingrove.

INTERVIEWS

Anderson, Dave, Museum of Flight, Seattle, WA, January 20, 2018.
Armstrong, John, via Teleconference, February 18, 2020.
Ballard, Chuck, Museum of Flight, Seattle, WA, January 20, 2018.
Belshaw, Paul, via teleconference, August 6, 2020.
Bogash, Bob (Boeing, retired), Museum of Flight, Seattle, WA, May 12, 2015.
Booth, Murray, Museum of Flight, Seattle, WA, January 20, 2018.
Christensen, Zac, Museum of Flight, Seattle, WA, January 20, 2018.
Condit, Dr. Phil, via teleconference, June 20, 2018.
Cumming, Don, Museum of Flight, Seattle, WA, January 20, 2018.
Davis, Robert, Museum of Flight, Seattle, WA, January 20, 2018.

Dulski, John, Museum of Flight, Seattle, WA, January 20, 2018.

Delmar Fadden (Boeing, retired), Museum of Flight, Seattle, WA, December 13, 2015.

Florsheim, Bruce, Museum of Flight, Seattle, WA, January 20, 2018.

Forester, Clifford, Museum of Flight, Seattle, WA, January 20, 2018.

Hindmarch, John, Museum of Flight, Seattle, WA, January 20, 2018.

Imrich, Thomas, Museum of Flight, Seattle, WA, January 20, 2018; Museum of Flight, Seattle, WA, January 18, 2020.

Jackson, Duane, Museum of Flight, Seattle, WA, November 18, 2018.

Johnson, Jim, via teleconference, June 20, 2018.

Kanellis, George, Rainier County Country Club, November 18, 2017.

Lentz, Rick, Museum of Flight, Seattle, WA, January 20, 2018.

Mahal, Avtar, Museum of Flight, Seattle, WA, January 20, 2018.

McIntosh, Bill, Museum of Flight, Seattle, WA, January 20, 2018.

Mitchell, Fred, Museum of Flight, Seattle, WA, January 20, 2018.

Morton, Peter, Museum of Flight, Seattle, WA, May 12, 2015, March 21, 2015, October 5, 2015, December 13, 2015, and January 20, 2018; via teleconference, June 20, 2018.

Ruggiero, Frank, via teleconference, July 31, 2021.

Taylor-Houtchens, Marlene, Bellevue, WA, January 21, 2020; via teleconference, June 20, 2018; Museum of Flight, Seattle WA, January 20, 2018.

Taylor, Steve, Museum of Flight, Seattle, WA, January 20, 2018.

Sutter, Joe (Boeing, retired), Renton, WA, October 5, 2015.

Taylor, Dick (Boeing, retired), Museum of Flight, Seattle, WA, May 12, 2015.

Timmons, Larry, Rainier County Country Club, November 18, 2017.

Wimpress, Jack, Bellevue, WA, January 21, 2020; via teleconference, June 20, 2018; Museum of Flight, Seattle, WA, January 20, 2018.

Wingrove, Flip, Museum of Flight, Seattle, WA, January 20, 2018.

INTRODUCTION

This book's origin began with the goal of writing the most in-depth and historically accurate volume on the development and operation of Boeing's 757 jetliner. This effort took me to the Boeing Archives in Bellevue, Washington, where I was assisted by corporate historians Michael Lombardi and Tom Lubbesmeyer. While there, I was given access to incredible quantities of information on this remarkable aircraft. Retired Boeing vice president and 757 flight deck designer Peter Morton assisted immensely by deploying his Rolodex, allowing me to make contact with the people who were there on the scene during the long gestation period of the Model 757.

The journey that ensued was nothing short of amazing. Speaking with 757 program leaders, designers, marketing managers, and pilots opened up avenues to the largely untold story of this airplane that really dates back to 1969, when the need for an improved version of the Boeing 727 was identified as being necessary. As they say, good things take time, and the 757's thirteen-year development led to an airliner that, at the time of its introduction, was the most fuel-efficient jetliner in existence. As we will explore, this was not at all at the expense of aircraft performance. The 757 was a spritely and responsive aircraft to fly, loved by pilots the world over. In this volume, I have made a concerted effort to include many quotes from the people who knew the 757 best, in effect letting them tell their story to the greatest extent possible.

The business leadership aspect of this aircraft development in also extremely relevant, not only to the aviation enthusiast but to business leaders in any industry. The people who spearheaded the 757 program, Dr. Phil Condit, Jim Johnson, and Jack Wimpress, explain in their own words how to develop a winning culture with a large group of diversified people. The team was markedly understaffed due to the concurrent development of the 767 wide-bodied jetliner, but this positive culture was successful in creating two major jetliners by one company during the same time period, something that many industry experts claimed was simply not possible.

In addition to the research-and-development story of the Boeing 757, we will also look at different versions of the aircraft, both conceptual and operational. Furthermore, we will explore the technical aspects of the 757, along with a detailed description of the airplane's flying qualities from veteran 757 pilots. With the intention of putting the reader directly in the pilot's seat of this amazing aircraft, a detailed walk-around inspection is also included.

The following pages tell the incredible story of the Boeing Model 757 and the impressive people who took part in its creation.

CHAPTER 1
THE LONG ROAD TO THE BOEING 757

The origins of what would eventually become the Boeing 757 can arguably be traced back to 1969. At the time, the Boeing 727 was gaining a reputation for being a capable performer and rapid seller. Having first flown in 1963 and grown into the stretched 727-200 by the end of the decade, the 727 set a new standard for jetliner performance, comfort, and operational efficiency. The Pratt & Whitney JT8D turbofan engine, purpose-built for the 727, was both quiet and miserly on fuel when compared against the existing jet engines of the day. Eastern Airlines even touted their 727s as "Whisperjets" to advertise the relative quietness of the aircraft. Yet, less than a decade later, newer high-bypass engines were being developed, which brought noise levels so much lower that the 727 "Whisperjet" soon found itself noisy by comparison.

As the 1970s approached, inflated fuel costs and the public-relations issue of jet engine noise came to the forefront. Many airports, including New York's La Guardia, for which the 727 design was optimized, were becoming ever more noise sensitive. Fortunately, due in part to the ongoing wide-body revolution, advanced engines that operated at

The Boeing 727 was an amazing success for Boeing and the airlines that flew it. The aircraft was popular because of its relative speed, efficiency, and quiet operation when compared with other aircraft, filling the short-to-medium-range role at the time. Boeing sold a total of 1,872 727s during its production run, which lasted from 1963 until 1984. The aircraft pictured (N8870Z, c/n 21288, l/n 1234) later served with Federal Express after being converted to a 727-225F freighter, operated as N464FE. *Courtesy of the Boeing Company*

markedly reduced noise levels with unheard-of fuel economy were already being developed.

As always, Boeing had its finger on the pulse of the world's airline customers and realized that in addition to the noise and fuel consumption issues, there was another driving force: the desire for even-greater passenger capacity. While the "stretched" 727-200 had debuted in 1967, still-further stretches were being actively studied by Jack Steiner, the central figure behind its creation.

THE 1969 727-300 CONCEPT

Courtesy of Jennings Heilig

General Electric was in the midst of developing high-bypass turbofan engines for both the Lockheed C-5 Galaxy military transport and the McDonnell Douglas DC-10 widebody jetliner, to lift them off the drawing board and into the sky. During 1969, Boeing explored the possibility of marrying an upsized 727 airframe with the new General Electric CF6 engine. This engine was substantially more powerful than the Pratt & Whitney JT8D engines in use on the 727-100- and 727-200-series airplanes, producing more than twice the thrust. Even with a generous fuselage stretch over the 727-200, it rapidly became apparent that the 727's characteristic center engine would not be required. Since parts commonality was still extremely important as far as production and operating costs were concerned, the basic 727 vertical-stabilizer structure was to be retained to the maximum extent possible while deleting the center-engine S-duct. That being said, additional structure would need to be added in the aft fuselage to suit the new, more powerful, and heavier engines.

The 727-100 shared the same basic wing design with the higher-capacity 727-200. This wing, brought forth by Joe

Sutter, was a masterpiece of high-lift design that gave the lighter 727-100 its impressive short runway performance. While the same wing was also effective for the 727-200, considering the shorter runways frequently in use at the time and the maximum takeoff weight increasing to 208,000 pounds from further stretching, a larger wing would likely be required. Although an improved wing was seen as the key to keeping takeoff and landing speeds low enough for the required short-field performance capabilities, the 1969 design was also intended to have as much commonality as possible, so an entire redesign was out of the question. The proposed solution was to retain the legacy 727 wing, but with an additional wing root insert on each side to provide the requisite wing area for the larger, heavier 727-300 design. Interestingly, this was precisely the same strategy that McDonnell Douglas successfully employed while developing the DC-9 Super 80 from the DC-9-50-series jets roughly a decade later. The main landing gear was to be installed in the new wing root structure, featuring a four-wheel bogie-type arrangement, adapted from the venerable Boeing 720. Although FAA certification was envisioned for late 1972, with no buyers the project was never launched. Boeing even tried offering the airlines a concept known as the 727-XX, which had its fuselage diameter increased to 188 inches. Ironically, while the twin aisles it offered were not en vogue in 1973, their ability to reduce aircraft time at the gate would be desirable today. Timing is everything in the jetliner world, though, and Boeing found no takers for its visionary concept.

Although the 727-300, and the 727-XX for that matter, may well have been ahead of their time, they were not ideal for the period. A serious downturn in the airline industry at the end of the 1960s and early 1970s led to little interest in the aircraft from airline customers. Boeing's commercial aircraft production in 1968 totaled 376 jetliners, but by 1972 this number had plummeted to just ninety-seven. Boeing's workforce was also drastically reduced from 148,000, to just 53,000 within the same time period. Realizing the bleak situation, Jack Steiner turned to improving the existing 727-200 Advanced. This airplane, thanks to the increased thrust available with the new -17 and -17R engines, allowed for the desired gross weight increase and made it possible to accommodate more passengers or more fuel for additional range (or both). While this assisted in reducing seat-mile fuel costs, which was one of the primary goals for the 727-300 project, the community noise issue remained unsolved. In fact, the JT8D-17 and -17R engines were slightly louder because of supersonic jet efflux, creating additional shock-cell noise. Even so, the 727-200 Advanced was extremely popular and significantly outshined the 737-200 in sales during this time frame.

THE 1973 BOEING 727-300

Courtesy of Jennings Heilig

Boeing's success with the 727-200 Advanced didn't stop the company's engineers from trying to achieve even-higher passenger capacities while reducing seat-mile costs. Steiner and his team looked for ways to accomplish this with minimal changes to the airplane. The concept that emerged in early 1973 was marketed as the 727-300 but was known internally as the 727-300-S15H. Their design featured a lengthened fuselage, with the entire stretch occurring in the center section, where the wing meets the fuselage, leaving the forward and aft fuselage sections largely unchanged. Again, like the 1969 concept, four-wheel main landing gears were added to the design that would utilize the same wheels and brake mechanisms as the 737 to support parts commonality.

Lift needed to be increased substantially for the aircraft to have good takeoff and landing performance, though, so a small amount of additional wing area was provided by 3-foot wingtip extensions and a revised inboard trailing edge. Unfortunately, this was still not nearly enough, so technology was drawn from the 747 program and its use

of variable-camber leading edge Krueger flaps. While the aircraft was in high-speed flight, they were stowed in the wing's lower leading edge, perfectly conforming to the camber of the lower wing surface. When operations required flight at slower speeds, though, a set of mechanisms deployed the Krueger flaps forward and up onto the leading edge, while also bending them into a more curved shape. Since they worked quite well on the 747, creating exceptionally good lift at low speeds, engineers surmised that using these 747-style high-lift devices would give the 727-300 the necessary lift for acceptable takeoff and landing performance. For airlines that desired enhanced takeoff and landing ability, but with a smaller aircraft, Boeing also proposed a 727-200B concept, using the fuselage length of the older -200 series aircraft in combination with the larger -300 wing.

Although a wind tunnel model showed a strong propensity for "deep stalls" with the modified wing design, Boeing continued to flight-test the concept, using the second 727-100 built (reregistered as N1784B) as a test bed. This aircraft was substantially modified with the wing extensions and variable-camber Krueger flaps. Flight testing discovered that one of the primary issues with this high-lift design was the aircraft's inability to handle situations in which one of the outboard Krueger panels was damaged or missing, leading to a significant imbalance of lift between the two wings. When testing was conducted with one retracted or missing, the aircraft had a tendency to roll quite sharply. The only way to mitigate such a catastrophe would be to install a larger number of smaller leading edge panels, but that solution required more extension mechanisms, leading to more weight and an overly complex system that would be difficult to build and maintain. Boeing's Dave Anderson recounted: "We had what was called a piano player leading edge, which meant that you had a little built-in fence between the Krueger locations on it. We decided that this might be beneficial to avoiding a tendency for the wing to pitch up during a stall. I remember in the wind tunnel, some of those configurations we were running 24/7. Alan Mulally

This is a wind tunnel model of the proposed 727-300. This model was found to have a strong pitch-up tendency during stalls and flight at high angles of attack. Note the extended wingtips and enlarged inboard trailing edge sections added for additional lift. *Courtesy of the Boeing Company*

was there on the nighttime shift, and I came in on the daytime shift, and we would always leave notes for each other. What Alan, who worked on Stability and Control at that point, had written in his notes was 'Best pitch-up configuration yet!' We immediately reported that the nighttime crew may have found a solution, not realizing that he was being uncharacteristically sarcastic! We immediately called management and said Alan and the nighttime crew have something great here, until we studied the data and found that we had more pitch-up than any airplane we had ever seen!"

The other handling deficiency caused by the new leading edge configuration, as applied to the 727 wing, was the increased tendency for the aircraft to continue pitching nose up when the wing approached a stall. This could even cause the airplane to flirt with the dreaded "deep stall." The modified aircraft exhibited this unwanted attribute even during landing tests, when the flying pilot was required to forcefully push the nose down while

flaring to land! These problems led to the testing of different leading edge device configurations, ultimately finding that a hybrid combination of slats and Krueger flaps resulted in acceptable handling. By June 1974, the best results were gained by using slats on the inboard leading edges and retaining the variable-camber Krueger panels on the outboard stations. Even with the improved lift and handling characteristics, the new wing, when mated to a fully loaded 727-300 airframe, would require an 11 knot higher approach speed compared to the 727-200 Advanced. Plain and simple, this meant the 727-300 required longer takeoff and landing runs unless weight, be it payload or fuel, was intentionally limited, resulting in the loss of profits, range, or both.

Boeing engineer Dave Anderson continues: "The 727-100 with the 727-300 wing and landing gear was tested over at Moses Lake. We could rotate really far because it was a –100 body length and a –300 landing gear. Combined with the variable-camber Krueger leading edge, we could stall it out in ground effect. That was pretty problematic because the wing was longer and the body angle was higher . . . I do remember unintentionally doing stalls in ground effect, resulting in the airplane setting back down on the center engine tailpipe. The engine didn't work very well after that, so we had to replace its tailpipe."

WHAT IS A DEEP STALL?

Wings create lift by having relatively low-pressure air flowing smoothly over the upper surface of the wing. As the angle of the wing relative to the passing air increases, lift also increases until the angle becomes too great for the air to "make the corner" around the leading edge of the wing. This leads to a breakdown of the smooth airflow over the wing, causing a loss of most of the wing's lifting ability. While pilots are careful to ensure that this condition does not occur during normal operations, still the aircraft must exhibit the tendency to pitch nose down when the pilot releases the nose-up control inputs. Many aircraft with T-tail designs similar to the 727's exhibit a nasty trait where the nose continues to rise as the high tail flies into the aerodynamic wake of the wings and side-mounted engine pods, disturbing the airflow over the horizontal stabilizers and elevators. This renders them unable to force the nose down despite the pilot's best efforts, and in extreme cases, it can be impossible to regain control.

Many of these aircraft require safety devices, known as stick pushers, to keep the aircraft from getting into this scenario. The "stock" 727 was better than most in this regard as it only exhibited this tendency with certain wing flap and spoiler combinations during flight testing. The establishment of an aircraft limitation prohibiting the use of speed brakes (spoilers) and flaps at the same time while in flight effectively made the 727's handling docile and safe without the use of the "Band Aid" devices required on other T-tailed aircraft.

There was also one more interesting effect related to the interrelation of the modified 727-300 wing and the aircraft's empennage, which was not an issue on the original 727 designs. The turbulent flow from the wing at high angles of attack caused the tail structure to flex. Dave Anderson was aboard many of these test flights and recounted the experience: "When we did high-altitude stall testing with our modified wing, we were aware of the tendency for the horizontal tail to oscillate during a stall as it is buffeted by turbulent flow coming off of the wing. So, we monitored strain gauges, and set limits on what movement we'd allow and still continue testing. The data showed us staying barely within limits, but we didn't realize until we landed that it was not symmetrical and was consistently exceeding our limits in one direction. We later removed the horizontal tail for inspection, and a photo exists somewhere of that airplane in a hanger with no horizontal tail. We bragged that we had finished our 'tail off' testing, which is common in wind tunnels but impossible in flight. Conveniently, we ended up with a video of the tail-walking shadow on the starboard wing when we were luckily pointed perfectly away from the sun."

Even with these challenges, Boeing engineers pressed forward, determined to solve each issue and produce an improved and more efficient 727. Concurrent with these research and development activities, Boeing's marketing department continued to communicate with the airline customers in an ongoing effort to build the ideal jetliner.

THE EARLY-1975 727-300B

Courtesy of Jennings Heilig

Airlines such as Braniff, Swissair, Trans Australia Airlines, United Airlines, and Western Airlines were beginning to show some interest in the project. The further "stretch" of the 727 airframe brought it into a size class where it was beginning to compete with the new wide-body Airbus Industrie A300, and, to some extent, perhaps even the Lockheed L-1011 and McDonnell Douglas DC-10. United, especially, was seen by Boeing as the key customer because the size of their potential order would justify launching the program, now known as the 727-300B.

The 727-300B, referred to internally as the 727-300-S125, was somewhat similar to the 1973 727-300 (727-300-S15H) concept airframe, but with a new version of the JT8D family of engines. This upgraded power plant, known as the JT8D-217, used the basic JT8D-17 high-pressure N2 spool, while incorporating a larger first-stage compressor (N1), expanded in diameter from 40 to 49 inches. This change made the engine more powerful by up to 21%, along with a specific fuel consumption decrease of 12%–16%. This was accomplished by having a larger volume of air bypassed around the engine core and mixed with the exhaust in the tailpipe. Aside from the additional thrust and fuel economy generated, it also considerably reduced the engine's noise signature except during the landing approach, which was found to be 2–3 decibels louder. While the aircraft, with the refanned engines, would allow compliance with Stage 2 noise rules at the time, more-restrictive Stage 3 rules were slated to be enacted in 1978. Due to this, these new engines would go from being considered "quiet" to "noisy" in just a handful of years. Despite that, the engine still solved most of the short-term issues that the 727 was experiencing from the standpoints of fuel burn and power.

Although it appeared to be the best compromise, it caused a major engineering headache when combined with the 727 airframe. Selecting an engine with a larger fan diameter, while still retaining the three-engine configuration, would require an expanded S-duct, which could be accomplished only through a major redesign of the entire tail section and aft fuselage. This had the potential to add significant development and production costs during a time of flat jetliner sales. To make the undertaking worthwhile, the new jet would have to perform well in terms of runway performance, noise, and fuel economy.

United set forth an interesting metric to evaluate the projected performance of the proposed 727-300B aircraft. The gauntlet was set to determine the airplane's ability to fly from Lehigh Airport, near Allentown, Pennsylvania, to Chicago O'Hare, with alternate airport fuel for a diversion to Detroit, Michigan, plus an additional one hour and fifteen minutes of reserve and contingency fuel. It is thought that United chose this scenario because it constituted a worst-case condition. Allentown's runway was quite short, requiring exceptional aircraft performance to carry the weight of a full airplane and generous fuel reserves. Boeing's George Kanellis was charged with making the performance predictions, given historical weather conditions at Allentown. Kanellis discovered that even with the most-powerful engines available for the airframe, statistically the aircraft could take off with a full cabin only 78% of the time in the morning. The afternoon departures, with higher average ambient temperatures, were much worse, at roughly 45%. Although this might seem extreme for a summertime situation, Chicago is oftentimes plagued by thunderstorms during the hot summer months, requiring ample alternate fuel reserves, generating higher takeoff weights.

Boeing engineer Larry Timmons summed up the 727-300 situation during the 1974 time frame: "The 727-300 was going to be all things to all people. It was going to have tremendous short-field characteristics, be as fast a lightning, and be kind of quiet. The JT8D-200s were not particularly quiet and mostly on the sideline . . . it was noisy. At any rate, I believe that program was killed by, number 1, the noise rule. Number 2, the airplane became everybody's pet project. . . . Some said, 'We don't need the ventral airstair anymore, so let's take that out. Well, now we have space in the back end, so let's do something about the S-duct,' and it rolled on from there. Finally, it became a new airplane. It lost sight of the original objective, which was a quick entry into an improved airplane. Obviously, the fuselage couldn't get any longer without putting a root insert in, so the gear could be bigger and longer. The whole thing was pretty much up against its design limits, so it was canceled."

By February 1975, United Airlines' chairman, Edward E. Carlson, was still deliberating the decision on the 727-300B. There were many dynamics in play within the airline industry at the time in the United States. Jet fuel prices were at record highs, eventually increasing from $0.12 to over $1.00 a gallon, and the world economy was volatile at best. Additionally, the Airline Deregulation Act was just around the corner, the effects of which were still unknown despite numerous "educated" guesses. Due in large part to these uncertainties, the final decision was delayed until August 28, when United Airlines elected to not buy the airplane.

THE LATE-1975 727-300-S68F

Courtesy of Jennings Heilig

For a short period after the United 727-300B rejection, one more radical modification was researched by the Boeing engineering staff. A new engine, viewed by many as a long shot, was being developed by a partnership of General Electric and SNECMA. It was called the CFM56, a conjunction of CF, which was GE's "Commercial Fan" line of engines, and "M56," which was SNECMA's commercial engine project. This power plant used the engine core of the General Electric F-101 engine developed for the Rockwell B-1A supersonic bomber program, combined with a larger-diameter, high-bypass fan section. Production was a joint venture, being conducted both in France and the United States. This engine promised to be quieter and more fuel efficient than the Pratt & Whitney JT8D-200-series engines previously considered. In fact, the CFM56 was destined to become one of the most prolific, reliable, and efficient jet engines in history. However, at that point in time, it was yet to sell in significant numbers, and the CFMI consortium was on extremely shaky ground. Further,

for the 727, the fan diameter increase from 40 to 60 inches was an even more monumental task, requiring a more drastic redesign of the aft portions of the 727 fuselage and empennage. Undoubtedly, with the earlier 727-300B exhibiting the deep stall characteristic, it is nearly certain that Boeing's Aero Staff was at least nervous that the larger, side-mounted engine pods would possibly have a negative effect on the airplane's low-speed stability and deep stall resistance, to boot.

After a short study, the 727-300-S68F was consigned to the dustbin and signaled the last advertised use of the "727-300" name, although future endeavors to create a new jetliner would still focus on "derivatives" of the 727 and 737 for several more years. Boeing's Bob Norton indicated that the entire 727-300 study and flight test program cost Boeing roughly $48 million. While this may seem like a needless expenditure, it was quite the contrary, since this sum is relatively inexpensive when compared to producing an airplane that does not fulfill its mission or is too expensive to build and fly. Boeing had done its homework and made sound decisions, but further studies were already in the works.

THE 7N7 EMERGES

By mid-1975, after the 727-300B's failure to launch, it became apparent that something more dramatic would be required to make a go of a new midsized jetliner. Boeing was already working on an all-new design known as the 7X7 (later to become the 767). This concept was a wide-body airplane, to be offered in a wing-mounted, twin-engine configuration as a domestic, "transcontinental" jetliner. Boeing's Duane Jackson wrote about the transition: "The 727-300 studies had gradually evolved from 1971 to 1975 into the 727-300B configuration, which represented the best design possible with three JT8D re-fan engines, but it was still not an ideal solution for United Airlines. An internal study was conducted all during the first half of 1975 with engineers from the new airplane 7X7 team working with the derivative study team. The intent of the study was to explore possible iterations of derivative concepts between the 727-300B definition and the all new 7X7 design. Six models were compared with varying degrees of new configuration elements. They included the 727-300B at one end of the spectrum and the 7X7 all new design at the other end. In between these end points were models that included additional body length, those with an all new wing plus aft mounted, high bypass engines, some with an all new wing plus wing mounted high bypass engines, and other variations, increasingly moving further away from a derivative concept to an all new design, represented by the 7X7 configuration. These designs were evaluated and compared on a consistent basis to illustrate their performance characteristics, as well as their economics, including cost estimates. The results of this study provided guidance in illustrating the powerful influence of incorporating a new wing with wing-mounted,

high-bypass engines. While the fuselage could be retained in a derivative design, it was clear the wing and engines needed to be all new to make significant strides toward being able to fully satisfy customer requirements.

Following the decision by United Airlines in August 1975 to not proceed with the 727-300B program, a new path was outlined for the derivative study team. This new direction included the decision to consider only those design concepts that included an all-new wing with wing-mounted, high-bypass-ratio engines. Starting in January 1976, the study team requested a new official internal model number for these follow-on studies from the Boeing Archives organization at Corporate Headquarters. Harlan Bracken, the official keeper of these internal designations, provided a new internal number, model 761-XXX, to represent what was externally called model 7N7.

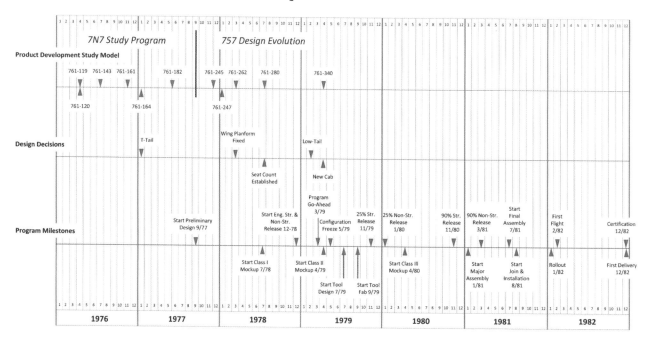

757 Development Milestones

Courtesy of Duane Jackson

MEET DUANE JACKSON

Duane Jackson joined the Boeing Company in 1961 after receiving a bachelor of science degree from Texas A&M University, where he majored in aeronautical engineering, and is a 1986 graduate of the University of Pittsburgh's Management Program for Executives. Mr. Jackson held engineering positions on the 727 design project, 737 aerodynamics staff, and product development until 1974, when he became configuration design supervisor of 707/727/737 product development. In this assignment, he was responsible for developing product improvements and derivative airplane designs to enhance the commercial airplane product line.

The role of the configurations group in the preliminary design process was to develop an overall airplane design definition by coordinating with the many project and staff disciplines to bring all the design elements together. The general-arrangement drawing, inboard profile, and other relevant drawings and descriptions were included in a configuration definition document. Performance characteristics, cost estimates, and economics assessments were evaluated by the supporting functions to determine the next steps in the development process. The interaction with potential customer airlines was also essential to plan further actions.

Various 727 derivative studies evolved into the model 727-300B, a major derivative design that had significant development until late 1975. From the lessons learned in that effort, derivative studies were undertaken, assuming the requirement for a new wing with high-bypass engines under the designation of model 7N7. These exploratory studies continued through mid-1977. Following the 7N7 studies, additional design work, along with continued interaction with potential customers, led to the evolution of the 757-200 design, and the program was launched in early 1979.

From 1980 to 1983, Mr. Jackson was the manager of configuration development in the 757 Division. During the

Courtesy of Duane Jackson

757 Development Program, he supervised Configuration Design, Project Weights Management, Configuration Analysis, and Sales Support groups.

From 1984 to 1990, Mr. Jackson was the manager, and then chief engineer, for 757 product development. He received the 1986 Ed Wells AIAA Award for managing the technical development of the 757 Package Freighter.

From 1990 to 2001, Mr. Jackson was the chief engineer of new airplane product development. He participated in major design studies, including the exploration of a potential 600-passenger New Large Airplane. He also worked with company-wide organizations to develop what became the high-speed, Sonic Cruiser concept, and the design concept that evolved into what became the model 787.

Mr. Jackson retired in 2001 after forty years with Boeing. He was born in Denison, Texas, and now resides in Bellevue, Washington. He and his wife enjoy golf and travel.

"N" FOR NORTON

It is noteworthy that Boeing typically did not want to confuse the media or traveling public by using a numeric designation in the "7 series" (707, 727, 737, etc.) for a study airplane that had not been authorized for offer or officially started by a launch customer sale. Peter Morton explains: "Sometimes the internal study designation was used (e.g., 761-XXX), and sometimes a letter designation. For example, the 7X7 designation was used at public air shows, which became the 767 when launched. Sometimes a letter chosen was the first initial of the last name of the engineering leader for the program; in this case, that of Bob Norton, who led the preliminary design for an airplane that became the 757 when it was launched. Another example from the mid-1980s was the 7J7, a technology demonstration program to develop process and technical innovations that would emerge on the 777. The "J" stands for our leader on that program, Jim Johnson, who had served as the 757 director of engineering. Once launched, a program typically underwent a significant metamorphosis, it got a number, and was assigned a team with new leaders and a tremendous increase in resources necessary to move from conceptual product development and preliminary design into a full-blown production program."

FUEL-EFFICIENT POWER

The use of fuel-efficient, high-bypass turbofan engines, which were now in a second generation of development, was seen as the ideal power plant for the 7X7. During this pre-ETOPS (Extended-range Twin-engine Operational Performance Standards) period, on the basis of the reliability experience of piston engines, the Federal Aviation Administration had a long-standing rule prohibiting the use of aircraft with two engines operating overwater more than sixty minutes from a suitable landing site, although a few foreign operators and the US military had been operating modern jet transports this way for years. Boeing saw the potential of the 7X7 to be more than just a trans-con airplane, though, and because of the sixty-minute rule, a three-engine version of the 7X7 was also envisioned during early development. Despite Boeing's optimism about the 7X7, management was still unenthused about launching the 7X7 simultaneously with another all-new aircraft due to the large expenditures, risks, and manning requirements involved. This meant the engineering staff dedicated to a 727 successor, by this time led by Boeing's Bob Norton, not only had to build a state-of-the-art airplane that customers would buy in quantity, but they also had to sell it to Boeing's upper management as a relatively inexpensive program.

The 7N7 program looked at all kinds of potential derivative aircraft. While most of these studies concentrated on modifications to the 727 and 737 airframes, no stones were left unturned. This model shows a 707-320-series-based concept with a stretched fuselage and high-bypass engines. *Courtesy of the Boeing Company*

THE COMPETITION: THE COOPERATIVE DASSAULT / MCDONNELL DOUGLAS ASMR AND THE ATMR

The bleak market, soaring fuel costs, and an unstable economy, combined with the rumblings of airline deregulation in the United States, created a dynamic where airlines were hesitant to make major commitments, even for an aircraft possessing moderate fiscal advances. McDonnell Douglas was also looking for a low-cost entry into the 150-seat market, which sat squarely between their smaller DC-9 series and larger DC-10 wide body.

The Dassault Mercure 100 was a French jetliner designed to compete with the Boeing 737 and, to some extent, the McDonnell Douglas DC-9. The Mercure used the same JT8D-15 engines optionally employed on both the Douglas and Boeing machines, but it had a higher passenger capacity. Although it was fast—in fact, faster than either competitor due to its advanced wing design—it was also heavy due to the large cabin design and high passenger count.

The Dassault Mercure 100 was a solid design: fast, reliable, and efficient. Unfortunately, it was a "point design" airplane in the truest sense. Optimized for capacity over range capability, the airplane's range was limited to approximately 600 miles with a full cabin. *Courtesy of Geoffrey Thomas*

Naturally, Dassault was predominantly influenced by the European market and projected that a full-cabin range of roughly 600 nautical miles would be sufficient. A common misconception among historians is that the Mercure was range-limited by its small fuel cell volume . . . not so. It was a classic payload-limited airplane, but just taken to the largest extreme possible. The airplane actually had the volume to carry 32,520 pounds of fuel with fewer passengers for long-range operations, or a full cabin for just over 600 miles. The JT8D-15 was the only viable engine in the required thrust range during the early 1970s, thus severely limiting the Mercure's ability to carry plenty of fuel and a full cabin on the same flight.

The airplane itself was described as a "pilot's airplane," exhibiting fighter-jet-like handling and leading-edge technology, neither of which was surprising, since Dassault was the company behind the Mystère and Mirage fighter jets. The Mercure was also the first jetliner to offer a Head-Up Guidance System (HGS), developed from the Mirage, which was useful in allowing the pilot to look outside while simultaneously viewing flight instrumentation.

Every aircraft design is a mixture of engineering-design compromises. The original Mercure 100 design sold only fourteen examples, while exhibiting operational efficiencies that were unheard of at the time. Speed and efficiency, at the cost of flexibility, was not the optimal design. This demonstrated to Dassault, along with the rest of the industry, that a good airplane can fail when the incorrect mixture of compromises is employed. However, Marcel Dassault was not a man to give up, and, realistically, he truly was on to something that could have been incredibly successful. The Mercure airframe, if mated to an efficient power plant with higher thrust and lower SFC numbers, would have likely been a real winner. Such an aircraft could carry BOTH passengers and ample fuel at the same time, leading to a truly flexible airplane.

Dassault attempted to gain support from the French government for the reengined Mercure program, but due to the huge losses on the Mercure 100, assistance was not forthcoming. Undaunted, Dassault went to McDonnell Douglas looking to form a partnership to build a Mercure variant with a larger wing, paired with the newly developed CFM56 engine.

This was a risky move for Dassault. Prior to the emergence of the original DC-9-10 design, which first flew in 1965, Douglas invited SUD of France to bring their Caravelle jetliner for inspection, with the definite possibility of a partnership. The idea was to produce the Caravelle airframe, replacing the aircraft's early turbojet Rolls-Royce Avon engines with General Electric CJ-805 turbofans to create an efficient, quiet (but perhaps not very fast) entry into the short-range jet market. This aircraft, with its aft-engine design, had also inspired the Tu-134 with some "pressure" from the Soviet premier Nikita Khrushchev after a pleasant and quiet demonstration flight during a visit to France. Douglas looked at the aircraft extensively but eventually declined the partnership. Soon thereafter, the DC-9 emerged with a remarkably similar aft-engine configuration, likely leading to some questions about Douglas's business practices at the time. While Mr. Dassault would have

been aware of these risks, he would have also known that there was no other source of funding.

The Dassault / McDonnell Douglas venture reached the point of early marketing and became known as the Advanced Short-to-Medium Range Airplane (ASMR). This aircraft had incredible potential, but unfortunately no one with the funding ability recognized this at the time. The Mercure design, combined with the CFM56 engine, would have been very similar in size, speed, and efficiency to the future Boeing 737-400 and Airbus A320, the first of which would not fly for more than a decade hence. If this airplane would have been built, it would have been a windfall for both Dassault and McDonnell Douglas, with an incredible production lead against Boeing and Airbus. Alas, this was not to be, because both the French government and McDonnell Douglas were too financially risk adverse at the time. This was likely a large mistake and a different decision might have prevented the sale of McDonnell Douglas in 1997.

Quite similarly to their earlier endeavor with SUD on the Caravelle, McDonnell Douglas elected not to form the partnership with Dassault and instead to design a similar aircraft of its own. This concept, known internally as D-3243-2, was marketed as the Advanced Technology Medium Range (ATMR) airplane. This aircraft was similar in configuration to the Dassault design but incorporated a twin-aisle, six-abreast fuselage width. The ATMR was clearly designed to fit squarely between the narrow-body Boeing 7N7 and the wide-body 7X7, possibly killing two birds with one stone. Commonality on the ATMR

Dassault wished to partner with McDonnell Douglas to build and market the Mercure 200 as the ASMR. Marcel Dassault is pictured third from the left. *Courtesy of Geoffrey Thomas*

was obviously being explored with a cockpit design that was similar to the DC-10, adapted to the narrower fuselage. The size of the design also filled the large gap between the smaller DC-9-50 and the jumbo DC-10, effectively replacing the earlier Douglas DC-8 series. With the ATMR, McDonnell Douglas could market a "family" of modern jetliners to fit the needs of virtually any major airline.

McDonnell Douglas nurtured a long relationship with Delta Air Lines, which had, at one time or another, operated most of the commercial aircraft types produced by Douglas. Delta also realized that the merged McDonnell Douglas was suffering financially and would have preferred to purchase the McDonnell Douglas jetliner at this point, a move that was extremely tactical. Helping to keep MDC competitive with Boeing would spur price competition between the two manufacturers, naturally reducing aircraft and spare-parts prices. To foster this dynamic, Delta expressed interest in

In an attempt to counter Boeing's 7N7 program, McDonnell Douglas proposed the ATMR, which was marketed to many airlines, such as California's Pacific Southwest Airlines. Delta Air Lines expressed interest in purchasing the aircraft, but since additional potential orders did not materialize, the project was canceled. Delta later became a major customer for the Boeing 757. *Courtesy of the Boeing Company*

being the launch customer for the ATMR, which was now becoming known publicly as the DC-11. An order for sixty aircraft was possible to get the program running, but McDonnell Douglas wanted to have a second customer to make the program fly. Unfortunately for MDC, a second airline coming into the mix did not materialize in time, partially because of some strategic pricing on the part of Boeing. Delta was willing and able to wait well into 1981 to move forward, giving MDC time to assess and perhaps even secure another order. Boeing knew the best way to sell the 757 was to ensure that the DC-11 was never built. Offering bargain-basement pricing on the 757 (about $1 million below list price) as a limited-time offer to Delta clenched the deal and stole MDC's only customer away from them. On November 12, 1980, Delta announced that it had made a deal with Boeing to purchase sixty Boeing 757s for the tidy sum of $3 billion. Delta executive Robert Oppenlander expressed Delta's viewpoint on the DC-11 situation: "They wanted to launch a new airplane without taking any risk. That ain't the way it works!"

Two primary factors were in play, as indicated by Sandy McDonnell, who had taken the reigns of the company following the death of his uncle, James McDonnell. First was not desiring to compete head on with another aircraft, nearly identical in nature. McDonnell Douglas had made this error when they built the DC-10, which was directly competitive with the Lockheed L-1011 in a market that could barely support one such aircraft. Their ATMR was set up to repeat this going head-on with the 757 and 767. Second, Sandy McDonnell, in an interview with *Newsweek*, said, "We know our competitors are telling the airlines that we're not serious, but it isn't true. We just need more than one order. We want a clear airline consensus on what is really needed."

One other factor that may have been in play, leading MDC to turn away from the risk involved in producing the DC-11, was that US airline deregulation was changing the way airlines viewed aircraft capabilities and capacities. The 757/DC-11-sized aircraft was not necessarily desired by all airlines, with some feeling that the aircraft might have been too large for some of the markets. Sometime after the debut of the 757, program leader Jim Johnson had the opportunity to talk with Southwest Airlines' CEO Herb Kelleher during his tour of the Renton assembly hall and recounted the conversation: "Herb came up to visit, and I took him out to the factory to show him the Five-Seven. Herb was extremely complimentary of the airplane. He said, 'This is a great airplane. It is going to do really well.' And so I said, 'So, Herb, when do you think that Southwest is going to be ready to buy the Five-Seven?' Because we knew that as airlines grew, they had to have bigger airplanes. Herb looked at me and said, 'Never.' I still remember to this day, that was the moment that I began to believe that there was something else going on and that point-to-point frequency [was] going to end up being the dominant characteristic. It was that discussion with Herb that kicked me and caused me to think about it more. We were perfectly proud of the airplane…he said it was a great airplane, but Southwest didn't need it."

An overabundance of caution at the wrong time led to the end of the Dassault Mercure 200 (and the ASMR), which was slightly smaller than the emerging 757. While this aircraft would have likely been quite successful if produced, both the French government and McDonnell Douglas had individually and effectively snatched defeat from the jaws of victory. Sandy McDonnell's assessment of the head-to-head competition of the larger ATMR/DC-11 with the 757, in a market that would eventually yield orders for just over 1,000 jets, may have been quite sound. In any event, this signaled the end of the MDC effort to compete directly with the 757, while they concentrated on improving both the DC-9 and DC-10 airframes. Ultimately, this led to the production of both the DC-9 Super 80 (MD-80) and, a decade later, a stretched DC-10 derivative marketed as the MD-11.

The Farnborough Airshow, held annually in Hampshire, England, was the venue for Boeing's momentous announcement in 1976. Boeing submitted press release S-1775, which detailed the modern aircraft concepts, known as the 7N7. These first 7N7 concepts featured an all-new wing design but would still employ the fuselage dimensions utilized on the 737 and the forward body of the 727. The 727 cockpit and nose structure were also retained to promote commonality. Three different versions were envisioned, accommodating 120 to 180 passengers with a range capability of 1,500 to 2,000 nautical miles. The engines considered complementary for the design were the General Electric / SNECMA CFM56 and the Pratt & Whitney JT10D, which were under development. The larger, longer-range version could possibly use the proven Rolls-Royce RB.211 or General Electric CF6 engines, both of which required an optimized (slightly smaller) fan diameter.

Dean Thornton, Boeing's VP of finance, felt that a sizable customer base for the new airplane existed, justifying additional work on the project. Further, Joe Sutter was quoted as saying, "We have no pressure from anyone to touch this [Boeing narrow-body] cross section." This is not surprising, because making the 7N7 larger would certainly provide unwanted competition with the wide-body 7X7 along with substantial kickback from Boeing management. Norton was quoted in the *Interavia Airletter* as stating that the projected market for the 7N7 was roughly 1,000 machines. His prediction would prove to be nearly exact.

On October 4, 1976, *Interavia Airletter* 8601 was released, giving further details and providing drawings of the three 7N7 size classes. Looking at the drawings supplied, the design encompassed a fuselage-mounted horizontal stabilizer, with a vertical stabilizer seemingly based on the 737-200 design. This was the earliest venture away from the 727 T-tail design, negating the deep stall tendency that was a constant concern during the 727-300 studies. One of the primary design goals was to provide an engine-out cruise altitude of at least 12,000 feet at maximum continuous thrust on the remaining power plant. This would provide greater route flexibility in high-terrain environments such as Central and South America and ensure operational capability out of high-altitude airports.

Courtesy of Jennings Heilig

The most compact 7N7, the model 761-119, was intended to accommodate approximately 125 all-tourist class passengers comfortably on flights up to 1,300 nautical miles.

Courtesy of Jennings Heilig

The midsize 7N7 aircraft, the model 761-120, was designed to carry 180 passengers over a nonstop distance of 1,600 nautical miles. This variant would utilize the same engine type (possibly with a slightly increased maximum thrust) and wing planform.

Courtesy of Jennings Heilig

The largest of the breed during this period was named the 761-143, offering a projected range of over 1,800 miles while transporting 180 passengers. This design bore several differences from its other stablemates to allow the higher

operating weights required. Impetus was to be supplied by either the General Electric CF6-32 or the Rolls-Royce RB.211-535, both of which were derivatives of larger engines already in service. The wingspan was expanded a further 7 feet, 1 inch to provide the necessary lift increase.

As late as 1977, the 7N7 was being publicized as a "737 derivative," using the cockpit, tail, and fuselage cross sections, presented in periodicals such as *Popular Mechanics*. The 7X7 was also in a state of change, showing photos of a very L-1011-esque aircraft in a tri-engine configuration. Both designs would continue to evolve.

An interesting aspect of the early 761 designs was how similar they were in appearance and capacity to the later 737NG series of aircraft, which became wildly successful in the post-Deregulation era. It is noteworthy that both the eventual 737NG, and to a greater extent the 757,

The 7X7 was a wide-body design that was to be offered in two versions: a domestic twin jet and an intercontinental trijet. In the mid-1980s, ETOPS certifications made the trijet option unnecessary, though many of the systems of the eventual 757 and 767 aircraft still derived from this configuration, having "left," "center," and "right" architecture. *Courtesy of the Boeing Company*

Many of the early 761 concepts bore a strong resemblance to the later 737 Next Generation series aircraft introduced in the 1990s. *Courtesy of the Boeing Company*

would both surpass their originally envisioned capability goals. Both went on not only to possess transcontinental ability, but to become the primary jetliners in use from the West Coast of the United States to the Hawaiian Islands under Extended-range Twin-engine Operational Performance Standards (ETOPS) rules.

As time progressed into 1977, airlines were interested in the narrow-body efficiency, though some wanted more passenger capacity to get lower seat-mile costs as well. Because of this, the 7N7 concepts slowly grew in capacity, largely due to the requests of British Airways and Eastern Airlines. Duane Jackson explains: "So, we went from 150 seats, to 162 seats, to 177 seats over a period of feedback iterations and presentations, and then [we would] stand back and think about what was possible. We got to 177 seats, and the airplane was really good on seat-mile cost."

While this aircraft growth looked very appealing to the airlines during this time of economic uncertainty, a substantial amount of concern was being generated at high levels inside Boeing. Joe Sutter, who was the leader overseeing both the 7X7 and the 7N7 programs, began to express concerns that the size of the 7N7 (which was originally a 150-seat concept) had grown to a size where it could conceivably adversely affect sales of the larger 7X7. This was an undesirable effect that would defeat the purpose of producing two new airplanes during the same time period. In September 1977, Sutter decided that both the 7N7 and 7X7 programs needed to be redirected, and he took a fresh look at the designs of both aircraft.

In early 1977, the T-tail made a reemergence with concept 761-164 as the design moved away from the 737 influence of the early 7N7 program. *Courtesy of Jennings Heilig*

Over the ensuing few months, the 7N7 and 7X7 engineering groups stepped back to reassess their designs. The reflection period, enacted by Sutter, would eventually create substantial changes in both aircraft designs, since neither design was ideal in juxtaposition to one another.

The 7X7 team, seeing that the airlines were looking for greater fuel efficiency while keeping the wide-body comfort level, came up with a novel idea. Originally, the 7X7, which was to be the first model of a new family, had an eight-abreast fuselage, which offered the desired roominess but resulted in relatively high fuel burn. The design team saw that reducing the fuselage width to a seven-abreast design would be the best compromise, satisfying both requirements. This did lead to some complications, however. Jackson explains: "Unfortunately, this new seven-abreast cross section didn't have the capability of having two LD3 [cargo] containers down below, because it takes an eight-abreast cross section like the A300 or the DC-10. So, Row Brown invented an LD2, which was narrow but the same height as the LD3. Nobody had ever used it because it hadn't been invented yet, but the LD3s were widely used throughout the world. We, the company, rationalized that we will sell enough airplanes that the LD2s will be used throughout the world. The main thing is that it got a more efficient airplane. So, they showed this to United as a much-better airplane, better direct operating costs, better operating empty weights. This became the baseline 7X7. This was happening from September 1977 to early 1978. The airplane program got redesigned into a seven-abreast airplane. United said, 'OK, that is what we will do.' So, we launched the program in early to mid-'78, and it became the 767-200 airplane, with 211 passengers. In the meantime, Joe Sutter said to Bob Norton, 'You go back to 150 passengers like I told you initially, two years ago. Back to 150 passengers and start over.'"

Due to this directive from Sutter (150 passengers in a three-class layout with generous seat pitch), the 7N7 team made major revisions to their design. As we have already seen, the early 7N7 concepts were based largely on the 737, with all-new wings, power plants, and a three-crew cockpit. In the months following the 737-based designs shown publicly in October 1976, the size increases requested by airline feedback made the 727-based designs more attractive. The model 761-182, with 177 seats, was a 727-based derivative with favorable economics. This "reflection" period caused significant concept changes that would define the eventual production 757. Boeing published the internal *Derivative Program Review* document on November 23, 1977, introducing concept 761-245. This design was an attractive airplane that combined many differences from the early 761 (737-based) designs. Most importantly, because of the direction from Joe Sutter, the passenger seating was reduced to 150 passengers (low density, mixed class) so as not to compete directly with the 7X7/767. An all-new wing, spanning 114 feet, 11 inches, with a modest sweep angle, was thought to be the most efficient option when paired with twin, wing-mounted, high-bypass turbofan engines. The main landing gears were of a two-wheel design, since the airplane was to be quite light for its size. The design was also leaning toward a two-crew cockpit during this time period, using the 737 cockpit platform, in contrast to the earlier three-crew concepts. The engine options were similar to the pre-1977 concepts, utilizing the optional Rolls-Royce RB.211-535, General Electric CF6-32, or the Pratt & Whitney JT10D, each of which was designed to produce approximately 32,000 pounds of thrust each.

The projected still-air range of the 761-245 was 1,650 nautical miles versus the 2,280 nautical-mile range of the 727-200 Advanced. Clearly, British Airways' short-range requirement was having an effect on the design at this point, since they had indicated that they were interested in the lightest-weight aircraft possible. This would also meet the one-stop transcontinental range requirement that was set for the aircraft at the time.

THE 7N7 BECOMES THE 757

As the late 1970s came to a close, the concepts swung back toward the 727 design in a few significant ways, one of which would eventually stick. A look at 7N7/757 concept model photos from Boeing news and advertisement releases shows the airplane in a state of identity crisis. The horizontal tail was depicted in some as a T-tail, obviously borrowing back from the 727, while previous 761 studies called for a conventional tail layout.

The other challenge for Boeing was that the two perspective launch customers for the 757, Eastern Airlines and British Airways, were not in alignment with each other's wishes. British Airways wanted their machine to be as light as possible. Because of this, they desired a main landing gear with two wheels, which could theoretically save an additional 500 pounds in weight. Eastern, on the other hand, wanted an airplane that could have size flexibility and also be able to operate within the confines of La Guardia's restrictive taxiway loading requirements. The only way to make the 757 legal for operations in and out of La Guardia was to install four-wheel trucks. Eastern's position on the issue was that Boeing needed to solve the La Guardia problem, while the New York Port Authority indicated that they would need additional funding to increase the weight-bearing capabilities of their taxiways, many of which were over water on pilings. Boeing, painting outside the box a bit, sent personnel to assist with the runway engineering project and to help provide funding.

Dr. Phil Condit remembers the situation: "What we were really trying to do in Bob Norton's team was to satisfy the requirements of the airlines. We talked to British Airways and Eastern a lot about the 767 (or the 7X7 at the time), and from our standpoint, talking about the product development, was that we were less interested in a second model as we were to satisfy their requirements and make sure they were going to buy a Boeing airplane. I can remember meeting with Lord King at British Airways. Lord King said, 'Gentlemen, I don't care what the airplane looks like as long

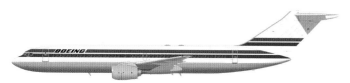

Immediately after the transition from the 7N7 study program to the 757 design evolution in early December 1977, concept 761-245 was explored. *Courtesy of Jennings Heilig*

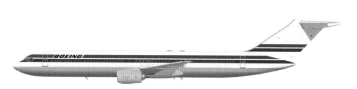

By mid-January 1978, concept 761-245 had grown slightly with a small stretch to the fuselage and was known internally as concept 761-247. *Courtesy of Jennings Heilig*

Dr. Phil Condit became the 757 chief project engineer during the program's redirection. *Courtesy of the Boeing Company*

as we get a configuration that seats 200 passengers and satisfies all of our requirements.' Eastern said, 'I want the airplane to fly into the same airports that the 727 goes into.' With those kinds of inputs, we started to massage the 727 and all of its possible configurations."

Boeing's ability to mix the needs of diversified customers has served their products and customers well throughout the company's history, avoiding the construction of an aircraft that is more "point designed" by nature. The Dassault Mercure fell notoriously into this category. The Mercure, designed solely for short-range European operations, was a good, safe aircraft that lacked market flexibility and was thus terminated after a short production run of just fourteen aircraft. This sort of financial failure can have fatal effects on the manufacturer, a situation that must be avoided at all cost. Condit continued: "I think this is really important. . . . One of the reasons that I believe Boeing airplanes have been successful is that you have these competing demands. The Europeans have tended to look at range requirements in a very different way—we don't need to go very far. We have to do London–Rome, and it is meeting those compromises that ends up making a great airplane. I think this is a perfect example. Had we gone with just the British Airways view, the airplane would have been an underperformer."

INITIAL ENGINE OPTIONS FOR THE 757-200

THE GENERAL ELECTRIC CF6-32

General Electric, in particular, was enthusiastic about providing an engine for the 7X7/757 project. Their concept engine was a derivative of the CF6 engine in use on the McDonnell Douglas DC-10, with the fan diameter reduced to 74 inches, while still retaining a similar core to the original CF6 version. During this period, Boeing also explored the possibility of the launch of a new 737-300 version using the new CFM56 engine that GE was building in partnership with SNECMA of France. The short-legged 737, however, would require a smaller fan diameter than the CFM56-2 that was currently under development. Ironically, GE was more interested in building the larger engine for the 757 program and saw the 737/CFM56 pairing as a comparatively low-production product. Boeing struck a deal with GE that the CF6-32 engine would be offered as an option on the 757, provided that they would also be willing to produce a CFM56 variant that could be compatible with the 737-300 airframe. The deal was struck, and GE agreed to produce both engines. In hindsight, General Electric's perception of the profitability of the two engines was quite ironic. Boeing would go on to sell thousands of CFM56-powered 737s, while never selling a single CF6-powered 757. This was likely due to the CF6-32's relatively high specific fuel consumption (SFC) of 0.643, compared to a projected 0.601 for the Pratt & Whitney offering and 0.641 for the RB.211-535C. Fuel prices were still very high, and fuel efficiency was king; hence the continued success of the narrow-body airplane, even today.

THE ROLLS-ROYCE RB.211-535C

The Rolls-Royce RB.211-535 featured a three-spool design, though turbofan engines typically have only two. The first of these offered on the Boeing 757 was the -535C model, capable of producing 37,400 pounds of thrust at sea level with a temperature of 84°F. Due to the fact that this engine was a lower-thrust derivative with a fan section reduced in size to 73.2 inches, the -535C featured a relatively low bypass ratio of 4.2:1. This led to a fairly high SFC when compared to Pratt & Whitney's projections for its all-new PW2037, which would become available in October 1984. Rolls-Royce was also working on a new RB.211-535 derivative, projected to have similar performance numbers to improve efficiency and aircraft range. Please see "Increased Engine Efficiency" on page 86.

TEX BOULLIOUN AND FRANK BORMAN MEET

In late August 1978, Boeing's president, Tex Boullioun, traveled to Miami, Florida, for a meeting to firm up specifications for the emerging 757. There, he met with Eastern Airlines' leader (and former Gemini and Apollo astronaut), Frank Borman. Together, they were whisked away on a four-minute car ride around the airport. Borman got down to brass tacks straightaway and declared that he wanted a 175-seat airplane (using a higher seat density than what Sutter was using in his metrics) and that if Boeing would build it, he was in. Boullioun reportedly said, "You've got it!" By the time the car had stopped, aviation history was made, with both leaders assuming sizable risks for their companies. It is noteworthy that both Eastern and Boeing had been communicating throughout 1977 and early 1978, so this was not a knee-jerk decision, but more of a carefully assessed determination made independently on both sides. On August 31, 1978, Eastern and British Airways submitted orders for a combined forty aircraft, totaling roughly $1 billion. The following day, on September 1, Boeing created the 757 Division and the 767 Division, which would be based in Renton and Everett, respectively.

Duane Jackson, who was involved in the development programs for the 727-300, 7N7, and eventually the 757, explained one of the ways the manpower issue was handled: "So, here we are . . . two airplane programs within six months of each other. There are not enough engineers at Boeing to design two new airplanes once you realize this low-cost derivative is no longer a low-cost derivative. It is not feasible to hire enough engineers to do all of that. So, let's make them (the 7N7 and 7X7) common so as to minimize the engineering requirements."

The liberal use of the word "derivative" was deliberate among the staff who saw value in the new aircraft and desired to see it move forward. To Boeing management, the word "derivative" was synonymous with "inexpensive to build." In this way, the team had a dual goal, which explains the way the 757 (née the 7N7) was ultimately developed.

The design that emerged from a clean sheet of paper on the drawing board was an attractive airplane; more 727-centric by nature. The design retained the dimensions of the forward- and aft-fuselage lower lobe from the 727, and initially the T-tail structure made another revival. It is important to note that Jack Steiner, the mastermind behind the 727, still had quite a bit of influence over the project, and he had an affinity for the T-tail design because of the aerodynamic efficiency it provided. The horizontal stabilizer, operating up high in relatively undisturbed airflow during normal flight operations, was more efficient and could thus be made smaller. It was projected that a fuel reduction per seat-mile over a 500-nautical-mile flight would show a benefit of 35% (total with the T-tail, but also largely based on the use of the new wing and engines), with an attendant reduction of 11% in block fuel over the 727-200. This configuration most assuredly would reduce aerodynamic drag and fuel consumption, but there were other factors in play. Boeing's Jim Johnson explains: "When we were looking at the version of the 7N7 that had the T-tail, I will never forget one night I got a call from Jack Steiner. Jack was elated that we had this airplane with a T-tail because, in his mind, it was a reflection of the 727. He went on for about twenty minutes about all of the advantages of a T-tail versus a low tail. Jack Wimpress was doing a comparison of the two when we had lots of meetings. Then, the other interplay that happened at about that time, we had to start thinking about the 7X7 (or the 767). One of the questions was: What is the industry going

The 761-280 was the aircraft initially bought by British Airways and Eastern, though the design would continue to evolve. *Courtesy of Jennings Heilig*

Jim Johnson was the chief project engineer for the 757 program. *Courtesy of the Boeing Company*

Thornton A. "T." Wilson became Boeing's CEO in 1969 and remained in that role through the development of the 757 and 767. *Courtesy of the Boeing Company*

to say if one airplane has a low tail and the other one has a T-tail? Is there a conflict between the two? We spent a lot of time between T-tail and low tail."

Even with the significant influence that Jack Steiner wielded, there were other viewpoints, combined with the solidification of the 7X7/767 program, which was in full swing, that cannot be underestimated. Murray Booth explains: "We had another team in the commercial company doing the 7X7, which was a trijet, but not with a T-tail (although we did studies on that too). The 7X7 side, which became the 767, and this was under my watch,

decided with no reservations that the right way to do this airplane, even if it had three engines, was a low tail. We ended up with a friendly but internal argument between the 7N7 side and the 7X7 side. They wanted a T-tail, and we tried to show why it was a problem. I had the staff responsibility for both programs, but I didn't have much control over my underlings on the 7N7 side. They were taking their orders from somebody else. This actually got to be a really serious debate about imposing versus doing the right thing . . . T-tail versus low tail. I just couldn't tolerate a T-tail for the 7N7 . . . you don't do that unless you have to."

During this time, often referred to as the "refinement period," a new airplane is looked at in detail in order to head off problems, allowing for the most trouble-free design possible. Another factor was based on concerns with customer perception, since they might ask themselves, "Why is a T-tail better on the 757 airplane but not on 767, when the configurations are similar?" All of these dynamics

John K. "Jack" Wimpress was leading the 757 Tech Staff during the development of the 7N7/757. *Courtesy of the Boeing Company*

Ken Holtby was the vice president of new programs for Boeing Commercial Airplanes during the development of the 757. Joe Sutter later referred to Holtby as a "very, very good designer." *Courtesy of the Boeing Company*

were relevant when the tug-of-war between the T-tail and conventional tail design came to a definitive conclusion late one night at Jack Wimpress's drawing board. Wimpress recounted his chance meeting when T. Wilson, the CEO of Boeing at the time, paid him a visit: "Looking at the wind tunnel data, I tried to formulate things like once the airplane started to pitch up into a deep stall, the pilot would have X seconds to recognize it, and X seconds to respond, and then the airplane would pitch down. I had to play these criteria in to Ken Holtby. Ken Holtby had the job of seeing to it that the technology of the 757 and 767 were comparable. He didn't like those criteria very well, and I can remember sitting at a drafting table one time with the airplane model in front of me, looking at it and thinking about it. T. Wilson came by. T. and I had

been friends for a long time, and I told him that I was trying to make the 727 tail work on the 757. He commented, and this is pretty near a direct quote, 'I wouldn't bust my ass to save the 727 tail.'"

Ken Holtby was also favoring the conventional tail design by this point because of the stability issues inherent with the T-tail design. Wimpress continued: "Ken Holtby kept saying to me, 'Jack, you are trying to formulate your criteria around your configuration, and that's not the way to do it.' That was very good advice. So, I thought about that for a while. I came up with a criterion that said if the airplane is in trim, anything the pilot can pull into, he can push out of. Now, that is a very good criterion. I would use it on any airplane I look at today. The airplane is absolutely safe—he can't pull an airplane into an attitude that it won't come out of. Well, when I took that to Holtby, he said, 'Fine, that is a good criterion.' Well, that put the tail back on the body because a T-tail could never meet that criterion."

In February 1979, this established the low-tail configuration of the production 757 airplane, the advantages of which were threefold. In addition to the stability advantage and no concerns about the deep stall effect, there was also the desire for design commonality with the 7X7, which by this point was locked in as a conventional tail design. In fact, the same engineers who had just completed lofting the lines for the 767 aft body, led by Ron Ostrowski, used their skills to design the loft lines for the new aft body of the 757. The resulting design, with its gentle aft body shape, along with the retention of the 727-style flat pressure bulkhead, resulted in a large space for the maintenance of the horizontal tail jackscrew and actually increased the effective passenger capacity by approximately one seat row. Ostrowski would later become one of the chief engineers for the 777 program and eventually vice president of the program. The 757 vertical stabilizer was laid out to be the same as that of the 767 vertical tail, with a portion of the base removed. As the designs progressed, commonality would become more and more important from the standpoints of pilot training and similar structures. Third, there was a significant weight savings by using the low-tail design, because with a T-tail design, additional structure in the vertical stabilizer is required to bear not only the lateral loads, but also the vertical loads imposed by the horizontal stabilizer. Adding all of these factors together, the decision to make the 7N7 a conventional tail design was the path of least resistance, even if it was to the dismay of Jack Steiner. With the tail position set in stone, there were other design changes on the horizon.

THE ADVANCED TECHNOLOGY WING

The six-month gap between the 767 and the 757 allowed the latter to take advantage of a new technology in wing shape. The 767 program had already "gone firm" on their

AIRFOIL DEVELOPMENT

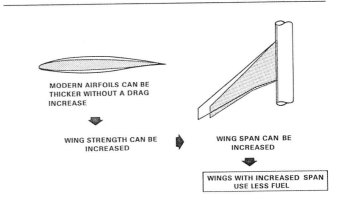

Advances in airfoil design led to the 757's 25-degree wing sweep. The deeper airfoil section reduced drag and increased fuel capacity, while negating the need for inboard ailerons and their attendant systems complexity. *Courtesy of the Boeing Company*

wing design, but it had come to light that with the use of a revised airfoil shape, improved drag characteristics could be achieved while substantially reducing wing sweep. In using this newly developed technology, there were three significant advantages gained:

1. Fuel capacity is increased by having a thicker airfoil section, since much of the aircraft's fuel is stored in the wings, leading to increased range and reduced bending loads on the wing. These two advantages alone lead to higher maximum gross weights and longer range with a lighter structure. Although not necessarily envisioned at this point, the ability for the 757 to fly not only transcontinental missions within the United States, but also transoceanic operations to Europe and Hawaii, with later ETOPS certification, was to become an enormous edge.

2. Less wing sweep allows for a higher-aspect-ratio wing while retaining similar or improved drag numbers. Because of this, the aspect ratio (wingspan divided by average chord length) can be increased, lending

itself to both greater range and better airport field performance.

3. Highly swept wings (such as those on the 707, 727, and even the "locked-in" 767 wing) display a unique and undesirable attribute due to the inherent flexibility of the wing structure. At high Mach numbers, outboard-mounted ailerons tend to "wag the dog," so to speak. This is because the force on the aileron hinges twists the trailing edge of the highly flexible wing, causing it to work in opposition. This phenomenon, known as "aileron reversal," causes the aircraft to roll opposite to the pilot's control input. This is why aircraft with highly swept wings often have the addition of inboard ailerons. This allows roll control at high speeds, because the torsion-producing outboard ailerons are (either mechanically or hydraulically) locked out during flight at higher airspeeds. The ability to eliminate high sweep, and thus the addition of inboard ailerons, is also advantageous for weight and systems simplicity on the 757.

All in all, there are some advantages to be gained by being slightly "behind" in schedule, and the 757 design team was determined to take maximum advantage of the latest technology. This being the case, the period from August 1978, when the airplane was first sold, until the official go-ahead in March 1979 was fraught or blessed, depending on the point of view, with major configuration decisions. Each was considered for solid engineering reasons, and each was taking the airplane further away from being a minor derivative and increasing cost and risk, potentially affecting schedule. Examples of such revisions include the following.

WING LAYOUT

The wing design was basically established from scaling up the 1,651-square-foot wing developed for the 761-245 (150-seat 7N7) by 300 square feet, arriving at 1,951 square feet, by directive from Joe Sutter. This would provide a low approach speed to compensate for having fan-only reverse thrust. At the time, it was envisioned that the airplane would replace 737-200s equipped with full thrust reversers, which were operating on short runways.

By keeping the wing sweep down to 25 degrees and the aspect ratio down to 8.0, the aileron reversal phenomenon of the 707, 727, and 747 was avoided, thus allowing an outboard-only aileron layout, which was deemed to be satisfactory by the Loads and Flutter staff. During the final configuration design of the wing and landing gear arrangement, it was determined that the landing gear trunnion (the upper member of the gear, connected with ball joints to the rear spar and the landing gear beam that rotates and allows the gear to swing up into the wheel well) was so short that it could be vulnerable to the phenomena called "gear walk." Gear walk is a cyclic vibration of the landing gear assembly (typically fore and aft) that most commonly manifests itself during heavy braking when the landing gear structure is such that it is not properly damped out. Bob Brown, a very experienced senior designer who was responsible for the design of the 767 landing gear, was particularly concerned about the ratio of the long gear and the short trunnion length. After several design options were considered, the decision was made to bend the rear spar forward from the engine location to the side of the fuselage, thus adding a few more inches to the trunnion gear length. This was satisfactory to Brown in that the design would be free from his "gear walking" concern. The fuel capacity was slightly reduced, but with the range requirements envisioned, it would not be a problem. The wing center section became 20 inches shorter, and the wheel well became 20 inches longer due to this rear spar revision. Fortunately, the longer wheel well turned out to have space available for the stowage of an off-wing escape slide for the "Overwing Exit Model" that Delta Airlines purchased later. Oftentimes, a design change made for one reason becomes serendipitous for other reasons down the road.

FUEL TANK ARRANGEMENT

During the design of the 757, a structures engineer suggested that the wing tanks be split into a "main" and "reserve" layout, with fuel management designed to retain a portion of the wing tank fuel in the reserve tanks until the airplane gross weight was reduced by fuel burn to a certain threshold value. This would reduce the wing-root-bending moment and allow a lighter structure to be used, saving, as Peter Morton remembers, about 700 pounds of empty weight. This arrangement was used in both the 707 and 747 airplanes. Peter Morton's flight deck group objected because it would complicate fuel management for the two-crew design and possibly require automation of fuel management if common procedures with the 767 were to be maintained. A detailed Study Engineering Work Authorization (SEWA) was launched to explore alternatives and resulted in a new fuel tank arrangement. The center wing tank end rib was moved from the wing root (its traditional location in most Boeing airplanes) outboard near the engine pylon, which moved the center of gravity of the wing tanks outboard to capture most of the proposed weight savings. This was a simple way to solve a complex problem, a technique later used on the all-new wing design of the 737NG series as well.

757 Fuel Tank Configuration

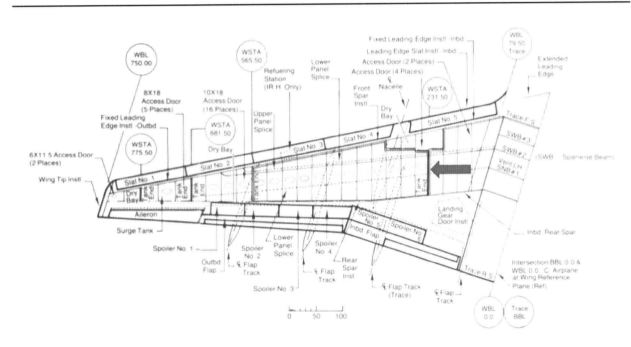

This structural drawing of the 757 wing highlights the fuel tank design. Prior to this point, most jetliners contained their center fuel tank entirely within the airplane's fuselage. Outlined in green and denoted by the blue arrow, the 757 center tank extended out into the wing, just inboard of the engine pylon. Since center tank fuel is burned first, followed by the wing tank fuel (*outlined in red*), this reduces wing-bending loads, allowing for a lighter structure. *Courtesy of the Boeing Company*

FORWARD CARGO COMPARTMENT

After the decision was made to adopt the more advanced 767 flight deck on the 757 (see "The Two-Crew Cockpit" on page 34), it became necessary to fit the much-larger volume of the aircraft's electronics, all of which required cooling with associated fans and ducts, into what had been essentially the relatively small 727 E/E bay located under the floor behind the nose gear. The solution required a significant reduction of the forward cargo compartment length and the relocation of the forward cargo compartment door. Given the need for a cargo loader (ground-handling equipment) to be able to clear the engine inlets, it was a challenge to locate the door with proper engine clearance, as well as a reasonable ability to have at least some space for baggage/cargo on each side of the door. Meetings with the customers were necessary to find an operationally acceptable configuration.

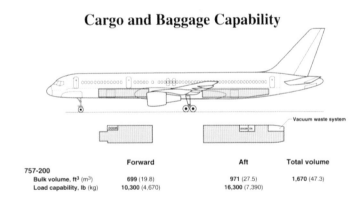

Cargo and Baggage Capability

Vacuum waste system

	Forward	Aft	Total volume
757-200			
Bulk volume, ft³ (m³)	699 (19.8)	971 (27.5)	1,670 (47.3)
Load capability, lb (kg)	10,300 (4,670)	16,300 (7,390)	

Courtesy of the Boeing Company

A view from inside the 757's E/E bay. Most of the aircraft's avionics and systems control computers reside in this cramped compartment, which is accessed from beneath the airplane through a hatch near the nose landing gear. *Courtesy of the Boeing Company via Duane Jackson*

CARGO COMPARTMENT DEPTH

Back in 1960, the 727-100 was designed with the relatively short aft cargo compartment, 10 inches deeper than the forward compartment, to enhance the weight and balance characteristics of the aft engine design. This design was carried through on the 727-200, which had both forward and aft body length increases. It was assumed to be the same situation on the 757, a 727 derivative sold to Eastern and British Airways in August 1978. Because the design was being drastically revised to become a low-tail, wing-mounted engine design, it was natural to consider revising the forward body to match the 10-inch-deeper aft body. After a necessarily short study considering weight and drag as well as economic potential benefits, the decision was made to retain the 727 forward lower lobe on the new design. The problem was that the economic analysis indicated there was no pricing value assumed for the increased cargo depth and the ability to carry cargo in standard containers.

There were also other forces at work. Initial wind tunnel testing showed an approximate drag increase of 1% with the use of the deeper lobe dimension for the forward fuselage on the 727. When Holtby considered that there was an estimated performance disadvantage, and no apparent sign of an associated marketing advantage, while taking into account the many design revisions that had already turned this "derivative airplane" into a virtually new design, it is said that he put his foot down. Given the information available to Holtby at the time, this likely seemed reasonable to him.

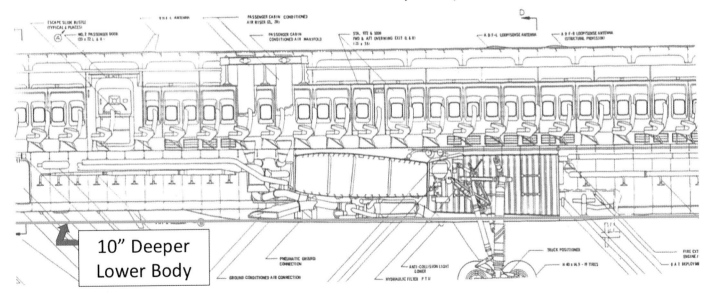

757 Forward and Aft Body Comparison

10" Deeper Lower Body

This inboard profile drawing shows the difference between the forward and aft fuselage lobe depths on the production 757. The ram air turbine (RAT), shown behind the main landing gear on the wing-to-body fairing, is noteworthy. *Courtesy of the Boeing Company via Duane Jackson*

Later, the truth of the matter became more apparent. Subsequent drag studies showed that there would have been far less drag increase had the deeper lower lobe been used. Further, the nose landing gear could have been made shorter, saving some measure of weight and wheel well space. The increased volume allowed by the smaller nose gear well and the larger lower lobe would have resulted in more space for the integration of the 767 electronics package and increased forward cargo capacity. The future widespread use of the LD3 "Short" cargo containers might have also been possible with a slight expansion of the baggage doors, leading to greater aircraft versatility.

AIRSTAIRS . . . PERHAPS NOT

The 727, 737, and DC-9 were offered with at least one airstair for passenger loading on the tarmac. Because the 757 was so high off the ground, it was a challenge to find space to store a telescoping airstair. During the continuing sales campaigns, it became clear that Alitalia Airlines in Italy absolutely required an airstair to operate on their routes. They operated their DC-9 fleet with airstairs at both ends of the airplane. After many iterations of layouts, including a radical scheme that John Johnson (the structures chief) said, in jest, that "we could charge people to watch it deploy." The design of this double-stack, telescoping airstair was deemed to be possible underneath the aft entry door. Following a study of the potential market for the airstair

requirements, it was decided not to offer an integral airstair for the airplane, and Alitalia went on to purchase the MD-80 design. In the meantime, the airports were continually updated to allow passengers to enplane and deplane without the need for a self-contained airstair, later deeming this feature largely unnecessary.

THE TWO-CREW COCKPIT

Up to this point, the 757 had been slated for a three-crew cockpit, derived from the 727 cockpit structure. As the design progressed, Phil Condit selected Peter Morton to be the lead designer of the cockpit on what was now being officially called the 757. Morton, who had been intimately involved

The Boeing 757 cockpit. *Courtesy of the Boeing Company*

with the 737 for many years as a marketing manager, came upon a new chapter in his career as the flight deck design manager. To simplify matters, Condit made it clear that Morton was to report to him directly. Since the flight deck designer traditionally reported to several people, because the cockpit is where all the aircraft's systems come together, this allowed him to "think outside the box" while focusing solely on the flight deck design. With Condit assuming this responsibility of coordination, Morton saw this as the ideal situation to create an industry-leading flight deck, especially since the crew complement dropping from three to two saved $0.03 per seat-mile. That may not seem like much, but it quickly adds up when considering a jetliner's speed.

Morton and his team of engineers began with the cockpit structure common to the 727 and 737, which lacked the "behind the panel" space to allow the use of the new cathode ray tube (CRT) technology. It was soon realized that the addition of a modern cockpit, using the available technology, could not be achieved with the 727/737 cockpit shell due to required structures behind the panel that could not be moved. The team then asked the question as to whether or not it might be possible to graft the 767's wide-body flight deck onto the narrow-body 757. Jack Wimpress recounts the situation: "I remember Ed Wells looking at the drawing one time, and he remarked, 'If you are going to copy a cockpit, it is a lot better to copy a forward-looking one, rather than a backward-looking one.'"

Avtar Mahal was the aerodynamicist charged with assessing the feasibility of such a daunting task. Mahal looked at the situation and found that with some measure of creativity it was possible, but there were challenges, both ergonomic and aerodynamic, that needed to be overcome. The solution to this problem was novel. By lowering the installation of the cockpit, placing it a few inches below the cabin floor level, the wide 767 cockpit could be grafted onto the narrow-body 757 fuselage. This step down into the 757 cockpit did cause some worry for Morton, who had to think of all the possible ramifications of every change. In this case he was concerned about crew members tripping over the step when entering the cockpit,

Peter M. Morton led the Flight Deck Group during the 757's shift from the 727/737-centric design to the modern 767-style cockpit. *Courtesy of the Boeing Company*

The task of grafting the already developed wide-body 767 cockpit structure onto the narrow-body 757 fuselage was an enormous design change, requiring significant ingenuity and thinking "outside the box." *Courtesy of the Boeing Company*

727 and 757 Cockpit Cab Comparison

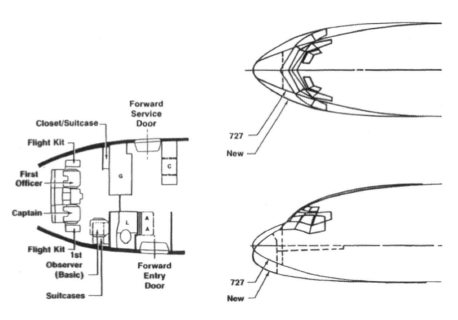

possibly even spilling coffee on the center console, over all of the aircraft's communication control panels. This was particularly significant because the entry into the cockpit on the 767 was a step up. Flight attendants and pilots would most certainly be cross-qualified on both airplanes, further exacerbating potential problems. Significant effort went into finding an adequate solution, which was ultimately to shine a light on the step that was bright enough for night operations, without being too bright and possibly projecting glare onto the pilots' windows. Although the step never caused a major problem on the line, it was somewhat common for crew members new to the 757 to nearly stumble on occasion.

Adding the wide 767 cockpit to the 757 also caused an aerodynamic issue. In mid-1979, wind tunnel testing showed that the curve above and behind the windshield was too abrupt, fairing the 767 shapes into the 757 fuselage. Just like with wing aerodynamics, air forced over a curved surface accelerates suddenly, in this case causing an area

of supersonic airflow across the region above the cockpit. This high-speed airflow not only would cause some measure of aerodynamic drag but would also significantly raise the cockpit's noise level.

Mahal, being a clever engineer, realized that if the floor of the 757 cockpit was canted down toward the nose at an angle of just 1.5 degrees, the curve above and aft of the cockpit windows could be shallowed enough to solve the problem and eliminate sonic flow when the airplane was at typical cruise speeds. In traditional Boeing style, studies were done to assess the effects of the slight cant of the cockpit floor on flight operations, which found there were no adverse effects for the pilots. In fact, there was actually a slight advantage, since the flight deck's orientation allowed 757 pilots to sight the runway a few vertical feet earlier than their 767 counterparts during low-visibility approaches. With these discoveries made, the cockpit shell design was solidified, though not without one last interesting effect. When the 757 team took the loft drawings to Joe Sutter during one of their weekly project meetings, he expressed concern that the nose of the airplane looked too much like that of the Douglas DC-8. Despite commenting on the similarity, he eventually approved the change, since he undoubtedly understood the reasoning behind it.

BIRD STRIKE

The 7X7, which by now was designated as the 767, had a six-month lead on the 757 and was well into the late design phases. New designs were continually tested as early as possible, to identify areas that needed improvement without having to unnecessarily retrofit production aircraft later. With a nearly six-month lead on the 757, the 767 nose structure underwent bird strike testing first. In these tests, a bird carcass is fired directly at the aircraft's windshield to test the integrity of the windshield structure. This time, things did not go quite as planned, since the bird-launching cannon missed the windshield, hitting just above it. This was a fortunate mishap because the bird broke through the cockpit cab structure, entering the test article's cockpit area. If this had happened in actual flight, it would have depressurized the cabin and, even more grievously, would have potentially damaged the electronics located in the overhead panel. Since these electronics control nearly all of the aircraft's systems, Boeing undertook an extensive redesign of the 767 cockpit structure, which naturally translated as an unexpected change to the 757 design as well.

Peter Morton and the flight deck design team took some risks and embraced technology, which served them well, but there was one instance where it caused additional difficulty, especially when the bird strike issue emerged. The change to the cockpit cab structure occurred quite late into the program. Flight at high altitudes causes the metal fuselage structure to become supercooled. Although the cabin environment contains fairly dry air due to the function of the air-conditioning packs, there is still some humidity, which tends to sublimate as frost on the inside of the structure. If no provision is made for this, when the aircraft descends into warmer air, the frost thaws and it creates quite a bit of moisture. All Boeing jetliners have drip shields installed that collect the water and send it to a bilge reservoir, preventing it from interfering with the aircraft's electronics. The de Havilland Comet 4, an early jetliner, did not have such provisions. Morton described a ride on a Comet as a Boeing engineer: "I passed my business card to the flight deck after takeoff and was invited to ride the jump seat. As we approached the top of descent for Piarco Airport at Port of Spain, Trinidad, the flight engineer opened a little bag and took out a towel, which he draped over the shoulders of the captain, then did the same for the first officer and himself. He offered me a towel and I politely declined. As we came down through 20,000 feet, it started to rain in the cockpit. I kid you not, a moderate drizzle ensued for several minutes. I then belatedly accepted the towel. The Comet had no drip shields, and the bare structure would build up visible ice on the inside from condensation, especially when the humidity on departure and climb was high."

Morton continued about the development of the 757 drip shields: "I have a story to tell because it got me in such hot water. It was one of those never-forgets! At this time, we were not doing much in the way of CAD/CAM, but everyone wanted to experiment with CAD/CAM, and so they came to me and said, 'We want to do the drip shields using this newfangled stuff called Computer Aided Design-Computer Aided Manufacturing, so how about that?' I had outsourced my drip shield design to Don Houck and to Jimmy Tsai, who were on the 707/727/737 division because we didn't have the resources. So, we ended up using this CAD/CAM thing and it didn't work. So, all of a sudden, when we would have Phil Condit's meetings inquiring, 'Are you on schedule with your drawing releases?,' Morton would stand up and say, 'No, I am not.' Today, that would have been a red light. The reason was that we put together this drip shield design that didn't work. The math was wrong. So, we went back into the mockups and did it the old-fashioned way and created the drip shields and everything was done. And then the

767 nose went into the bird [strike] testing. They fired a bird at the 767 nose, and it missed the windshield and hit the structure above the windshield and went right through it, which would scramble the brains behind the overhead panel. So, the 767 had to redesign the structure above. So, then of course our structures guy, John Johnson, had to redesign our structure to beef it up for the bird, and that meant the drip shields no longer fit, and I was back in the dog house with Phil Condit!"

Aircraft design is no place for the faint of heart!

CUTTING-EDGE AVIONICS TECHNOLOGY

It is important to note that design changes didn't always start with the 767 in Everett. There were times that the 757 drove changes on the 767. One such change that occurred in the eleventh hour for the 767 involved the flight deck avionics, since technology was rapidly progressing during this period. The 767 was initially to be equipped with early cathode ray tubes to present aircraft attitude and map displays. The installation volume required for these devices was accommodated by the 767's all-new cockpit structure. Further improvements were yet to come for the 757 flight deck. During this period in the early 1980s, the commingled technologies of computers and monitor screens were progressing rapidly. As a matter of fact, just the six-month lag of the 757 behind the 767 saw significant advances, particularly with filtered cathode ray tubes. These screens were originally to be monochromatic because they were bright enough to be seen in sunlight. Even these early displays would be quite an improvement over the old "steam gauges" previously used. While the 767 was in the design refinement stage, the induction of shadow mask cathode ray tubes into its cockpit occurred. These displays were leading edge technology and provided bright, vibrant colors. When the 757 flight deck team decided that these were the best equipment to install, the 767, late into its design refinement period, changed to match the 757's displays. This ended up making both airplanes better.

The colorful electronic flight instrument system (EFIS) display on the 757 was state of the art. *Courtesy of the Boeing Company*

MEET DEL FADDEN

The 757 and 767 cockpit teams had a secret weapon, embodied by an avionics engineer named Del Fadden. Fadden's involvement in EFIS-type flight instrumentation systems went back to the late 1960s, when he was working on the Boeing 2707 Supersonic Transport program. The EFIS concept was invented somewhat accidentally during the research-and-development portion of the soon-to-be-canceled Boeing SST program. Up until this point, attitude indicators were mechanical by nature, employing spinning gyros for stability and accuracy. Jets of the period required pitch attitude precision that was measured simply in degrees. The Boeing SST design would need pitch accuracy measured in tenths of degrees, necessitating a much-larger mechanical attitude indicator for the required pitch attitude "resolution." Fadden realized that this would call for a mechanical instrument that would be so big as to protrude out of the nose of the airplane. He elected to solve that problem later and, in the interim, just simply substituted the potentially enormous instrument with a makeshift computer screen while they developed the rest of the flight deck.

As Fadden's work progressed, the team soon realized that his "makeshift" instrument was anything but! Although Boeing's SST program eventually was discontinued due to environmental concerns and the emerging 1970s oil crisis, many of the research-and-development technologies worked out during the program went on to benefit future subsonic jetliners.

While EFIS was an outgrowth of the SST research experience, its use on subsonic airplanes was an outgrowth of human-factors studies on flight crew utilization of colors

Delmar Fadden led the 757 Flight Deck tech staff and brought knowledge of EFIS technology from other Boeing programs as far back as the Boeing 2707 Supersonic Transport program. *Courtesy of Delmar Fadden*

in guidance displays. EFIS offered incredible situational-awareness benefits, incorporating a moving navigation map on a CRT. Prior to these map displays, the pilot was required to use bearing and mileage from navigation beacons to build a mental image of where the aircraft was in relation to a navigation point or the arrival airport. This used a lot of the pilot's "mental bandwidth" just to maintain situational awareness. In the modern EFIS-equipped cockpit, the aircraft's position is displayed, allowing the pilot to concentrate on other tasks, increasing safety and significantly reducing task saturation.

The 757 adopted other traits from the 767 cockpit. As the 7X7/767 design was becoming more solidified in the mid- to late 1970s, the revered cockpit designer Harty Stoll took charge of the 767 flight deck team. Stoll had been deeply involved in the two-crew cockpit evolution for the Boeing 737, which introduced ergonomics, the likes of which had not yet been seen in the industry. The 767 design on the table during this period was the twin-jet "domestic" version, since the future ETOPS rules (see ETOPS, page 95), which allowed twins to do long-range oceanic flying, were not in existence yet. This meant that there was still a distinct possibility that the intercontinental 767 trijet might be built.

Going back to the early stages of the 7X7 program, Stoll looked at the topic of engine identification from the pilot's standpoint. Boeing convention had always been to number the engines on the basis of their position from port to starboard. For example, on a 737, the left engine was "engine 1" and the right was "engine 2." One must keep in mind that if the same naming protocol was used on a trijet, it would make the #2 engine the center engine. To meet common pilot type rating criteria, actuating a control in one aircraft version should have the same function and effect as in the other. Shutting down engine #2 (right) in a twin jet would cause a markedly different situation for the pilot of a trijet who shuts down engine #2 (center). The twin would experience significant asymmetric thrust, while the trijet's thrust would remain symmetrical. This major handling difference aside, aircraft systems and checklists would also be affected differently, causing associated failures on different electric, hydraulic, and air systems. Stoll came up with the idea of breaking tradition and naming the engines on the basis of their location on the aircraft. Twin jets would have a left and a right engine, while the trijet would have a left engine, center engine, and right engine. Using this naming method, shutting down the left engine on both the twin and the trijet would have the same handling effect, and very similar systems effects as well. This is because the airplane systems controls such as generators and pumps were also renamed "left, center, and right." The only difference for the twin is that there would simply be no center engine. Even though Boeing never built the trijet version of the 767, largely due to the introduction of ETOPS rules, this engine-naming method wasn't just applied to the 757; it has been standard on all subsequent Boeing twin jets.

A typical EICAS display during nominal aircraft operations at ground idle power. The inclusion of the N3 gauge on the lower display is indicative that this aircraft is Rolls-Royce RB.211 powered. Note the small "Bluegrass" Vs displayed on the lower portion of the upper display. This indicated to the crew that EICAS was attempting to display information on the lower screen. If that lower screen was blank, this would immediately alert the crew of a display failure, and an alternate mode could be selected. *Courtesy of the Boeing Company*

ENGINE-INDICATING AND CREW-ALERTING SYSTEM (EICAS)

The 757 introduced a system called EICAS to aviation. The Boeing managers who led three diverse teams to design the system were Delmar Fadden (tech staff), Donald "Sandy" Graham (avionics), and Peter Morton (flight deck). The following are their reflections on EICAS development:

For many pilots and copilots around the world, EICAS is a lifeline of vital information about the condition and performance of their Boeing aircraft. Its full name is "Engine-Indicating and Crew-Alerting System," and it presents as a stack of two cockpit displays in the center instrument panel, where engine gauges previously resided. EICAS is deliberately designed not to call much attention to itself except when needed to provide the flight crew with actionable information as required. It was first installed on the two-crew 757 and 767 and formed the architecture for further evolution into such features as electronic checklists in later Boeing models. Most aircraft manufacturers have adopted an EICAS on their aircraft; the Airbus version is called "ECAM."

Today, well into the twenty-first century, society is increasingly "instrumented," with pervasive information and automation available for personal, home, and automotive use. But forty years ago, at the dawn of the 757 and 767, pulling massive amounts of information together on a colorful screen was relatively novel.

For the groups we led that helped create EICAS in the 1975–80 time period, it was much more than a display. Born of a unique convergence of new hardware, human-factors research, and design innovation, it would make the 757 and 767 easily manageable by two pilots. This reflected a major step forward in two-crew design work that began with the 737 in the 1960s, when the Federal Aviation Administration first required that crew

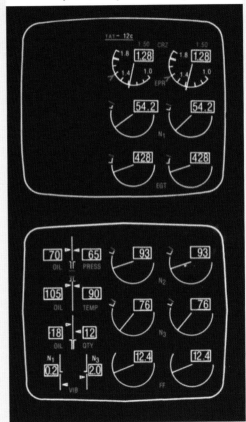

EICAS Full-Up Display (Rolls-Royce RB.211)

Courtesy of the Boeing Company

workload be rationally measured and tested as well as subjectively assessed, as part of the certification process.

EICAS was a significant production and procurement challenge, created in record time starting long after other 767/757 avionics systems. Developed by a hand-picked, dedicated Boeing and Rockwell Collins team, EICAS is an early example of a meticulously designed graphic user interface (GUI), executed with care to manage human factors, latency (time delays), and expected outcomes. Latency, the time between an action and the expected result, is important on a display. Humans are intolerant of delays over a few tens of milliseconds and tend to "push the button" again, with some impatience and irritation. That's a factor we tolerate with smart phones, not an acceptable aspect of airplane design.

EICAS was fashioned during a period of technology and labor union transition—flat-panel displays didn't exist yet, but cathode-ray tubes (CRTs) were like tiny color television screens that offered a flexible, versatile, and robust replacement for electromechanical gauges and other instruments that had dominated cockpits for decades. CRTs were originally qualified by the FAA for the 767 as primary attitude and navigation displays. The 757, which trailed the 767's development by about six months, adopted the 767's navigation displays to create EICAS and took the lead by using these CRTs to integrate the display of engine instruments and airplane system crew alerts. This was EICAS, and it became a first for transport-aircraft design installed on both the 757 and 767.

EICAS presented engine and airplane systems data in a "smart" actionable context to provide flight crews with critical information and to support decision-making. A digital computer using a massive connector with hundreds of pins to acquire data from sensors all over the airplane for processing and display, EICAS and its sensors were occasionally the butt of friendly jokes; one cartoon referred to "the left rear lavatory flush motor meter monitor"—which, of course, did not exist.

Boeing had conducted prior research into how flight crews could manage their workload with the assistance of technology (much of this work was accomplished in the NASA 737 Terminal Configured Vehicle [TCV] program).

This was a time of controversy regarding crew complement, involving airlines, pilot unions, manufacturers, and a US government task force studying flight safety history of two- and three-crew airplanes. The original 767 design was for a three-crew complement, whereas the 757 was launched as a two-crew airplane. Using 737 experience as a baseline, the 757 program explored ways to improve flight crew tasks, and EICAS became a significant feature managing crew workload of a two-crew design.

Boeing's leadership took a long view toward the potential for the 767 and 757 to have a common pilot type rating, for which display commonality was a critical factor.

Given the flexibility of CRTs formatted by a digital computer to present information in color, EICAS provided capabilities not available in traditional electromechanical engine instruments. With EICAS, pilots would know more of what was important and less of what was unimportant, and had to memorize less too. They could react more quickly because information could be presented in an intelligent context rather than as just an array of gauges. The flight deck and human-factors experts took advantage of this, using software to drive logic that filtered out distractions in certain flight phases. For example, during takeoff, EICAS suppressed information that might distract a pilot from flying the airplane. This was accomplished by managing which EICAS messages would be allowed in this phase of flight, and by keeping the lower screen off, called "blanking" the screen. It takes a very serious sequence of failures to warrant EICAS pulling the pilot's attention away from flying during these phases of flight. Aural warnings were integrated to ensure immediate pilot attention when needed.

Under normal conditions, once the engines are running, pilots have no need to monitor secondary engine parameters, such as oil pressure, rotor speeds, vibration, and fuel flow, so they can be blanked. In fact, the whole lower display remains blank. If a parameter enters a cautionary range or operating limit, it is brought to life to catch pilot attention, much like an oil low-pressure light on cars.

Color is used effectively but sparingly to convey a need for attention or action. If an engine parameter approaches a limit, the affected previously blanked instrument and its other-engine counterpart will appear and trigger an appropriate color change to attract crew attention. When a crew

member has only a certain amount of time to accomplish a task, EICAS will change the color of information—showing amber as a deadline approaches, and red if it is reached.

The application of human factors to EICAS followed a new "less is more" paradigm. Engine displays, previously dependent on complex mechanical designs (sometimes called "steam gauges" by pilots), were simplified almost to the point of austerity. Information is presented on screen in a familiar form of the analog indication that EICAS replaces, though with many scale markings eliminated in favor of colored limits. Numerical-value readouts are reserved for conditions requiring a precise response from the crew. An important goal is giving pilots a predictive cue to allow them to move the thrust levers to a "commanded" thrust level and then direct their attention elsewhere, knowing that the engine will, in several seconds, erase the command sector on the instrument as it reaches the commanded thrust level. There are many other important parameters displayed either all the time or as needed.

EICAS design decisions were based on a great deal of human-factors study, simulation testing, and application of new administrative tools. It would have been easy to provide too much information and, perhaps, display it at inadvisable times. To provide discipline and manage the airplane systems being developed by thousands of engineers at Boeing and suppliers, we created a Crew Systems Integration Document (CSID) to ensure consistency across all airplane systems and among all manuals and procedures that would later be used

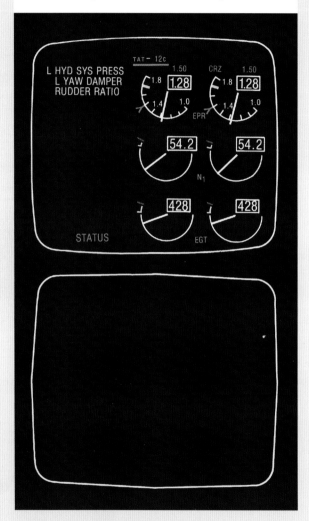

EICAS Cruise Mode
(With Crew Alerts)

Courtesy of the Boeing Company via Peter Morton

by flight crews as references. On the basis of detailed analysis of all pilot tasks throughout a flight, our flight deck designers used the CSID to govern EICAS functional design.

The original 767 three-crew, message-based alerting was enhanced and integrated into the EICAS, and it became the means by which airplane systems problems come to flight crew attention. Careful structure was built into the alert messages so they would be easy to interpret, and appropriate actions or checklists could be expeditiously consulted when needed. EICAS proved valuable during flight test, where potential problems often emerge. Sometime before certification was complete, another cartoon made its way through the hands of engineers and test pilots. It showed the lower EICAS display with a garish bullet hole, and the upper display with this alert: "DON'T SHOOT THE MESSENGER."

EICAS evolved to include many features that facilitated airline operations. It provides status of airplane systems to support flight crews during dispatch, it "remembers" fault messages to assist maintenance troubleshooting, and it facilitates interaction between flight and maintenance crews at the gate, where timely decisions will maintain operational schedules.

EICAS pioneered a fundamental change in airplane system design; pulling the system together was possible because the three "inventors" had a rich mixture of relevant skills, experience, and perspectives, with interdisciplinary backgrounds covering expertise in avionics, human factors, and airline flight operations and pilot training. We worked together with a high degree of mutual respect and had support from senior management on both programs who were risk tolerant and provided resources we needed. Most important was the talented team, whose creativity and industry completed EICAS design and development in roughly half the time normally allocated for a major new airplane system. There are a number of unsung heroes: lead engineers Walt Partel (software), Ed Farhner (hardware), By Bowman

EICAS Symbols: Primary Thrust Displays

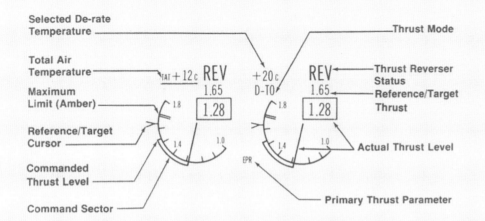

Selected De-rate Temperature

Total Air Temperature

Maximum Limit (Amber)

Reference/Target Cursor

Commanded Thrust Level

Command Sector

Thrust Mode

Thrust Reverser Status

Reference/Target Thrust

Actual Thrust Level

Primary Thrust Parameter

Courtesy of the Boeing Company via Peter Morton

(flight deck), and Frank Ruggiero (functional requirements), accompanied by a host of engineers who took responsibility for bringing a fully functional system to the flight test program on schedule. The 757 and 767 project pilots, Tom Edmonds, John Armstrong, and Kenny Higgins, along with many experienced training pilots, were vital to keep the design focused on pilot-centered actions and responses. With a tight schedule and no fallback alternative, we benefited from close partnership with the supplier, Rockwell Collins, who understood the challenge and assigned top-notch personnel to the project. Program success was a direct result of this close-knit intercompany working relationship at every level.

EICAS was, for the three of us, a committed engineering adventure. It changed the industry norms of how pilots, mechanics, and airline operations interact with the airplane, perhaps for all time.

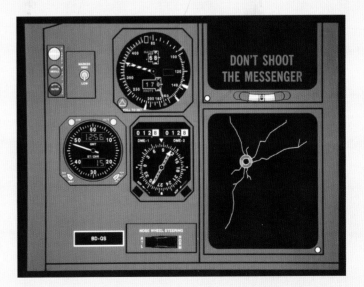

One of the important tenants of the 757 program culture, displayed on this humorous EICAS display. *Courtesy of the Boeing Company via Peter Morton*

757 PROGRAM LEADERSHIP AND CULTURE

The culture of the 757 program in particular was a unique step forward in a company already famous for execution of complex air transport programs. The 767 program launched nearly six months earlier and naturally had taken on most of the available engineering staff. This left the 757 team somewhat understaffed, requiring creativity and a unique culture to be successful in producing a top-notch airplane on time.

One strategy used in the 757 program was to put some of the engineering loads on the program partners and supplier companies, but not in an external fashion as is often done by corporations today. Boeing instead asked to "borrow" about 1,000 of these engineers and bring them to Renton, on a temporary basis, to assist with the design of the aircraft. These skilled people were not directly employed by Boeing but were admitted into the strictly controlled facilities with special identification badges. This, in part, solved the engineering gap between the available and needed 757 resources.

Another strategy was to "insource" work to other Boeing organizations. Peter Morton remembered: "The 757 Flight Deck group sent engineering work packages to the 737 Flight Deck group, which at the time was mostly occupied in sustaining engineering for the vast 737 fleet in the field, since there was no new major 737 derivative under design during this period. The 737 Flight Deck Project named a supervisor, Jimmy Tsai, in charge of that work; Jimmy attended our 757 Flight Deck staff meetings and reported at functional meetings such as Weight Improvement Program (WIP) status sessions. Some of Jimmy's engineers joined the exclusive 757 Flight Deck softball team, which had a standing vigorous competition against their counterpart 767 team. The chief of Weights Staff, Jim Hutton, was fond of introducing the WIP meetings with corny poetry, all of which started with 'Roses are red . . .' An elegantly good-humored leader, Jim took pity on me, the 757 Flight Deck

senior project engineer, in weight-savings status reports. Because the Flight Deck work package was so small in weight compared to structures, electrical, and other engineering groups, he allowed me to report weight savings in ounces so the numbers would not seem so small. I'll be forever grateful!"

This combination of working together, whimsy, and team spirit was pervasive and partially compensated for the fact that the 757 engineers were scattered all over Renton, unlike the centralized organizations on other programs. This dispersed staff also pioneered virtual meetings long before the advent of an internet, using telephone lines and dial-up audio conferences."

Jack Wimpress, chief of the 757 tech staff, shares his views on the culture that was created by the 757 program leaders:

It was part of our basic philosophy. After we had gone through a lot of these design refinements, and Phil Condit, director of engineering by then, and Jim Johnson, who at the time was the chief project engineer, and I was head of the tech staff, and I can remember the three of us sitting down and saying, "How should we run this program? What is going to be our design philosophy?" We came up with these three rules that I have quoted many times:

1. Never shoot the messenger.
2. Make decisions at as low a level as possible. There are all kinds of advantages . . . it trains people and it relieves your top management to work on the tough problems (which is a big advantage).
3. We are going to work the problems, not each other.

Those are three awfully good rules, and it made for a happy design team.

The leadership set up by Phil Condit, Jim Johnson, and Jack Wimpress created a culture of teamwork and a drive to see the 757 program succeed. Creating a new jetliner is an incredibly complex endeavor, even under the best of circumstances. This team, being behind the power curve with regard to manning and dealing with major design changes rather late in the program, was definitely challenged. The change from the 727 to the 767 cockpit structure on the 757 is an excellent example of a late design revision. There had been many industry pundits who expressed doubt as to whether Boeing could produce two new types concurrently, but the reality is that because of the positive culture set forth by the 757 leadership, combined with a team that felt empowered and well supported, the 757 program was an amazing success. The schedule was extremely fast paced, and due to the determination of the entire team, the airplane was produced on time, in fact slightly ahead of schedule.

The 757 culture has been viewed by many as a "gold standard" for establishing cohesive, goal-focused teams. A decade later, when Boeing set out to create the 777 wide-body twin, Phil Condit and Alan Mulally established a culture by design, building on the 757 success as a starting point. During the 777 program, learnings from the 757 program were utilized and additional culture-building techniques were employed. Peter Morton expresses his viewpoint: "The 777 culture was reinforced by several important things. The first was 'Boot Camp.' On the 757, we had found that people joining a new program brought along the culture of their previous experience. So, Phil and Alan determined that each person coming onto the 777 would attend an indoctrination class where a purposeful culture was introduced. The next was frequent communication, including all team meetings. The leadership team met off-site regularly under the guidance of their own organization development 'shaman' to focus on the culture of the organization. There were many examples of an emergent unique culture. I was at the time responsible for Boeing training and documents supporting the 777 program; even as a satellite Customer Services organization, we felt the pervasive influence of the 777 'Working Together' principles and were motivated to exceptional performance and shared in the 777 pride. When our Pilot Operations Manual was complete, the lead editor and supervisor insisted on delivering the first copy personally to Alan Mulally, autographed by all the tech writers. We made the pilgrimage to Everett to Alan's office and made a delightful ceremony while presenting the Operations Manual to him."

The 777 project pilots John Cashman and Kenny Higgins abandoned the decades-long tradition of stenciling the first flight pilots' names on the side of the airplane and instead had an italicized script, *"Working Together,"* under the right- and left-side flight deck windows. Likewise, we named the 777 Full Flight Training simulator "Working Together" and posted the famous 777 program launch document on the simulator sign-in desk. I often refer to the 777 program as "Boeing's Camelot," because it epitomized, in my opinion, the pinnacle of how thousands of personnel in the program joined with those affiliated from both inside and outside the company in a unique culture to build the preferred product for our customers and for their customers—the flying public.

The "Working Together" slogan and mindset were inclusive of all involved—Boeing employees, airline representatives, contractors, and government administrators, all working toward a common goal. This certainly proved to be a successful strategy that sets an outstanding example of leadership, not just with regard to aircraft production, but in any type of business.

NO LONGER "A SIMPLE DERIVATIVE"

As the post-1978 7N7 design evolved, with each decision made, nearly every portion of the aircraft was modified, losing ever more resemblance to the 727 and 737 airframes upon which it was originally based. Throughout the course of 7N7/757 development, the design gained new wings, engines, nose and tail sections, and landing gear. Phil Condit remembers: "Piece by piece, decision by decision, all for really good, thoughtful reasons, things kept getting changed. Example: We discovered that under galleys, you ended up getting a lot of corrosion, and therefore you ought to be enameling parts in detail, before they were assembled to protect for corrosion. Well, that changes the part number. When we were done, there were no 727 part numbers on the airplane. Not one, and I made a somewhat facetious statement that I am going to put one 727 vortex generator on the airplane somewhere so that I can tell Joe Sutter that there are 727 parts on the airplane."

Instead, the 757 was designed as much as possible to share parts and commonality with the 767. Although much of the airframe is different, many systems and cockpit components are identical. This was a bonus for airlines that operated both types in their fleet, and minimized the sheer number of parts that must be purchased and stored in multiple locations. This, in combination with the later change of the 767 to a two-person crew and creating an approval of a common pilot type rating for both (see page 81), saved air carriers untold millions of dollars. This commonality also benefited Boeing, reducing research and development costs for many components that were shared between the two aircraft. Instead of "looking backward" for commonality with the 727 and 737, as originally envisioned, Boeing had effectively hit a home run by "looking forward" and seeking commonality with the new 767 design.

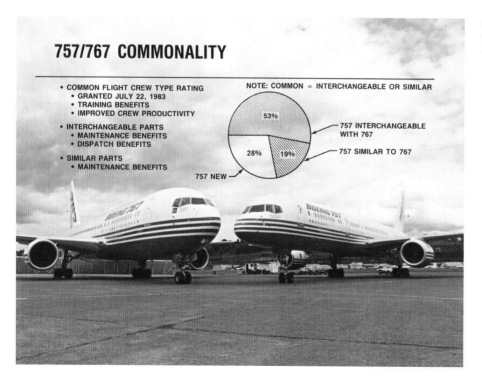

Commonality between the 757 and 767 aircraft was a major driving force for both designs. *Courtesy of the Boeing Company*

BUILDING THE PRODUCTION 757

After the August 31, 1978, launch orders were made by British Airways and Eastern Airlines, Boeing continued to seek improvements to their new airplane. As we have seen, the new design bore no similarity to the legacy 727 and 737 airplanes. Each common attribute was changed, one at a time, until the 757 was a completely different design.

The newly formed 757 and 767 programs, because of the desired commonality between the two aircraft, had to work together to achieve this goal. Changes were made to both aircraft to meet this purpose, particularly with mechanical components and cockpit design. The goals here were simple: reduce costs with parts commonality and make it a seamless transition for a pilot moving from one to another.

THE WEIGHT IMPROVEMENT PROGRAM

There was yet another large factor in development: weight. The less an aircraft weighs, the more fuel efficient it is, thereby allowing it to carry more passengers, more fuel, or both. The challenging part of this equation is that the safety and strength of the aircraft cannot be compromised. In order to accomplish this task, Boeing routinely sets up a Weight Improvement Program (WIP) on any new aircraft type, and the 757 was no exception. This team worked with each design group to reduce the weight of the airframe; the idea was that if weight was being contended with from the very beginning, it would save costly changes later while producing the most efficient aircraft right out of the box.

Regular weight review meetings were held, and support from the 757 team was high. There were approximately sixty design teams, each specifically responsible for a particular aspect of the aircraft design. The WIP meetings were enthusiastic, and those in attendance demonstrated the cohesive, team-oriented atmosphere expertly cultivated within the 757 program. Weight-saving modifications were submitted to the WIP group and were approved or denied on the basis of a ratio of cost-to-weight savings. It was not just the design groups that were involved. In the typical inclusive style of management that exists at Boeing, any company employee or contractor was welcome to submit weight-saving ideas for consideration.

The WIP program was highly publicized within Boeing and was featured in newsletters and posters distributed company-wide. Awards were given to employees who submitted a revision or suggestion that was adopted. Quarterly, the best ideas (not necessarily based on pounds, but on ingenuity) were celebrated at a banquet held at a local restaurant. This was also accompanied with an annual meeting to honor the top performers in the war against weight.

Substantial weight savings were made largely through the use of advanced material applications, such as the use of improved aluminum alloys to reduce the weight of the wing structure by 610 pounds. The use of composites such as graphite, Kevlar, and fiberglass saved an additional 1,100 pounds as well. Traditionally, jetliner brakes were made of steel and were quite heavy, but the 757 employed new-technology carbon fiber brakes that saved a further 650 pounds.

It is important to know that not all weight-saving strategies were adopted on the 757 program. The culture at Boeing dictated that safety and product quality could not be compromised, period. One such example is recounted by Boeing's Jim Johnson: "The 767 had picked a kind of wire . . . gauge of wire . . . and they were marching along. My guys came to me with a completely different approach. They wanted to use Kapton, and I went through review after review and it had a slight weight advantage. I was on the verge of making a decision to use Kapton. One of my mentors, Everette Webb, called me into his office and said, 'Jim, you are going to use the same wire that the 767 is using.' I said, 'But Everette, there is this weight advantage.' We were struggling with the weight of the airplane. He said, 'Well, there is a history here of this wire and problems, and so I want you to just use the same wire as the 767.' So, we

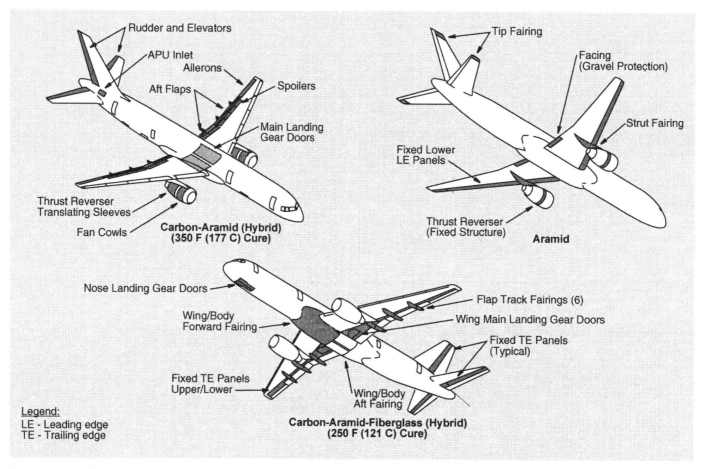

The use of composite structures to reduce weight and increase efficiency was extensive on the 757. *Courtesy of the Boeing Company*

did . . . and I did it just like that because I had so much respect for Everette. He had so much valid history, and he had been through so many decisions like it. It was one of those times that made the decision-making process fairly quick because he said, 'Go, do it.'"

Although not all of the ideas harvested made the cut, many were put into reality on the 757. As of December 1982, a total weight savings of 10,160 pounds was realized by the program through the acceptance of 1,410 suggestions.

This is enormous in the aviation world, since making the aircraft over 10,000 pounds lighter equated to markedly greater efficiency, allowing the aircraft to carry over an hour's worth of additional fuel, or significantly more payload on longer flights.

The road to the Boeing 757 was a long and winding one. The fuel crisis in the early 1970s, along with national and airline economies being in constant flux, made building the right airplane extremely difficult. The environmental

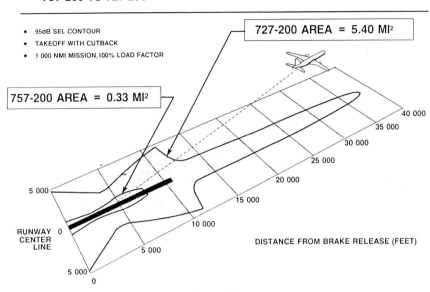

TAKEOFF NOISE AREA
757-200 VS 727-200

- 95dB SEL CONTOUR
- TAKEOFF WITH CUTBACK
- 1 000 NMI MISSION, 100% LOAD FACTOR

727-200 AREA = 5.40 MI²

757-200 AREA = 0.33 MI²

40 000
35 000
30 000
25 000
20 000
15 000
10 000
5 000

5 000
RUNWAY
CENTER
LINE   0

5 000

5 000

0

DISTANCE FROM BRAKE RELEASE (FEET)

Courtesy of the Boeing Company

challenges of noise and fuel burn also played a big role, as we have seen. Technical challenges, such as the small diameter of the 727 S-duct and the deep stall issue with the T-tail design, were also key factors leading to inevitable design changes. In fact, the airplane that pushed forward for production was the 340th permutation of the 761 design series, additional to the numerous 727 derivative studies done prior to 1975.

So many small changes and modifications had been made that the model 761-340, which would be built as the Boeing 757-200, was, in the end, an entirely new aircraft. This design was the result of nearly fourteen years of studies and refinements. By 1979 the aircraft was right, and, equally important, the time was right.

Courtesy of Jennings Heilig

CHAPTER 2
BUILDING AND FLYING
THE 757-200

BOEING PREPARES TO BUILD THE 757

Before the 757 Program even got its official go-ahead in 1978, Boeing was already seeking out subcontractors to produce both structural and systemic components. The 757 was composed of approximately 95,000 parts in total, many of which were manufactured by other companies. Tex Boullioun believed that European collaboration was important for foreign airline relations and useful to achieve some amount of risk sharing. He felt that as long as more than 50% of the airplane was produced directly by Boeing, the correct balance could be achieved.

Short Brothers, the legendary British aircraft company that produced bombers during World War II, was given the contract for the inboard trailing edge flaps and was one of several European manufacturers charged with component production. Further, British influence was also gained by choosing Rolls-Royce power plants for the early 757 deliveries. Without the UK's involvement in the 757, Boeing's launch sale to British Airways would have likely been a much more difficult sell.

British Aerospace (BAe) was also eager to get into the 757 mix and had a solid reputation for manufacturing advanced wing designs. In fact, BAe had manufactured the wings for the Airbus A300 and was the heir apparent for doing the same for the emerging A310 design. Up to this point, Boeing had typically built its own aircraft's wings, but with the shortage of labor because of the concurrent 767 development, and a desire for more British involvement, Boeing was serious about possibly breaking that tradition on the 757. Although Boeing and BAe had in-depth talks regarding this, the two companies differed on their visions for the partnership. Boeing wanted to have direct control and final say over the project, while BAe, on the other hand, wanted more of an equal partnership along the lines of their work with Aerospatiale on the Concorde. This dynamic led to Boeing Commercial Aircraft assuming the responsibility of manufacturing the wings as BAe fell by the wayside. Even though there was some concern that this parting of ways would have an adverse effect on the British Airways order, it would ultimately abide. Interestingly, there would still be some English involvement in the 757 wing structure, since de Havilland–Hawker was chosen to manufacture its interspar ribs.

The Airbus A310 was introduced as a slightly smaller derivative of the A300, launched with orders from Lufthansa and Swissair. The aircraft pictured is most likely F-WZLI (c/n 172), the second A310 prototype. *Courtesy of the Boeing Company*

The British Airways 757 deal led to an interesting effect, however. The governments of France and Germany became incensed that British Airways bought the 757 instead of the A310, leading to some question as to whether or not BAe should be given the A310 wing contract. Eventually, BAe did end up with the A310 contract and a 20% stake in the project because of two main factors. First, Airbus really needed BAe's assistance to produce the wing for their new airplane. Second, British Airways, quite tactically, announced that they would be more interested in the A310 if it were produced with a Rolls-Royce engine option. All of this was likely just political jousting and less about actually selling the A310 to British Airways, because a Rolls-Royce-powered version was never built, and the type was never operated by the carrier.

The 757 garnered cooperation with other American companies as well, with Fairchild, Grumman, Rockwell, Rohr, and Vought all being awarded contracts for various

The A300 was the first aircraft produced by the Airbus Industrie consortium. This twin-jet wide body first took flight on October 28, 1972. *Courtesy of the Boeing Company*

The "Class E" 757 mockup seen in the production configuration. *Courtesy of the Boeing Company*

components on the aircraft. These choices were solidified in October 1978, and contracts were announced totaling roughly $1 billion, resulting in a total of thirty-seven major contractors and hundreds of suppliers becoming involved in the creation of the Boeing 757.

On March 23, 1979, after thousands of hours of diligent work, the 757 design was solidified and the go-ahead for production was announced. The chosen concept for production was the 761-340 design, and this occasion began the forty-five-month road to the first aircraft delivery. Airframe construction of the first 757-200 (N757A, c/n 22212, l/n 1) commenced in December 1979.

By March 1980, the 757 and 767 designs shared many common features, such as the auxiliary power unit (APU), air-conditioning packs, cockpit components, windshields, and flight management, to name a few. However, there was an interesting difference between these two designs. In

This 757 mockup was used to evaluate interior installations. *Courtesy of the Boeing Company*

early 1980, the 767 was being sold as a three-crew airplane, requiring a flight engineer, while the 757 was being marketed as a two-crew airplane.

This created some contention with the pilots' unions, particularly with Eastern Airlines. The pilots' and flight engineers' associations were seemingly always at odds with their company's management. These union groups demanded that the 757 be a three-crew airplane. Boeing had a cockpit mockup of the 757 that was quite obviously a two-crew design. The Air Line Pilots Association (ALPA) had sent the Eastern Airlines MEC chairman to look at the mockup, when things got interesting. Reportedly, when the union representative sat in the mockup, he became red in the face, ripped the control yoke out of the floor, and handed it to the Boeing representative, along with a not-so-nice suggestion about where Boeing could put it!

While this incident was a demonstration of the highly contested subject of crew complement during the late 1970s and early 1980s, it was not the end of the order. A short time later, Eastern's vice president of flight operations, Capt. Buttion, visited Boeing. During their private meeting, he emphasized that the design team needed to protect the three-crew cockpit, at least for the time being. Because of this, Boeing provided a three-crew option if necessary to keep the Eastern order alive, though a decision still hadn't been completely agreed upon when the first metal was cut for the initial Eastern airplanes. In fact, those first aircraft had a right-side cockpit bulkhead that was 3 inches farther aft, so that a flight engineer position could be installed if needed. This arrangement also caused

Top: Shortly after first metal was cut on the 757 prototype (NA001, c/n 22212, l/n 1), the control cab section is readied for installation in early 1981. Note the white anticorrosive paint applied to the lower portion of the structure. *Courtesy of the Boeing Company*

Bottom: As indicated in this photo, the forward fuselage and cockpit sections for Ship 1 were completed on time and moved to final assembly. *Courtesy of the Boeing Company*

HOW TO BUILD A BOEING.

Boeing is now building an airplane that'll save millions of gallons of fuel: the new generation 757.

How much will it save?

A 757 flying 1.3 million miles a year will save 1.8 million gallons of fuel annually over the airplane it will replace.

Fuel economy has always been a concern to an airplane designer. Now it's more critical than ever.

Heading up one engineering group is Doug Miller. His specialty is preliminary design and development.

Doug and the design team were involved in the development of an airplane wing that has exceptionally efficient aerodynamics. It

would never have been possible if Boeing had not been testing and perfecting components of lightweight carbon-fiber and high-strength pure aluminum alloys.

Result: The 757 wing will get the airplane off the ground and flying with less fuel consumption than any airplane its size.

New aerodynamics, new materials, and engineering inventiveness along with a long-term commitment to constantly reach out and explore the unknown have made the 757 a reality.

Boeing believes almost anything is possible. Doug and the team are but one part of the immensely complex process that has helped create a future world of efficient commercial aviation — a step that can keep air travel one of the best values in the world of rising inflation.

THE BOEING FAMILY
Getting people together.

Courtesy of the Boeing Company

the flight deck entry door to have a jog to match the revised door frame, instead of being flat. Even to his own dismay, the payloads senior project engineer, Dick Ostlund, deemed the change necessary.

The 757 flight deck team worked for the next few weeks on the configuration, including the installation of a flight engineer seat and designing an appropriate workstation. Systems panels for fuel, hydraulics, air-conditioning, and electrics, originally intended for the pilot's overhead panel, were relocated, and a third cathode ray tube was also added to display EICAS information. The 757 electrical group, recognizing that the need for a three-crew configuration was likely a short-term issue, came up with an ingenious idea for the long term of the aircraft. They designed a wiring harness that had plug-ins at both the overhead panel and flight engineer's position. This allowed these airplanes to be easily converted from three-crew to two-crew airplanes by simply moving the control panels and reconnecting the harnesses. When Eastern finally decided on the two-crew 757 configuration, Boeing was able to eliminate the dual wiring harness, but it was too late to change the bulkhead position, making these airplanes unique to all other 757s.

An early 767 cockpit mockup featuring the flight engineer's station (*far right*). The first 767s were actually built in this configuration, but most were modified to a two-crew standard before delivery. Only five 767s flew in service with a three-crew cockpit but were all later modified to a two-crew standard. *Courtesy of the Boeing Company*

ANSETT'S THREE-CREW 767S

On the 767 side, the first several airplanes were built with a flight engineer position. The extremely late decision to change to a two-crew cockpit was made, and most of those first machines were converted with the dual-harness idea, initially devised by the 757 team and Harty Stoll. There were five early 767s that were actually delivered with a flight engineer's seat at the request of the purchasing airline, Ansett. For reference, these aircraft were VH-RMD (c/n 22692, l/n 24), VH-RME (c/n 22693, l/n 28), VH-RMF (c/n 22694, l/n 32), VH-RMG (c/n 22695, l/n 35), and VH-RMH (c/n 22696, l/n 100). It is interesting to know that because the FAA's 767 Type Certificate Data Sheet (A1NM) recognized only the two-crew version, these airplanes could not be operated by a US carrier with an FAA registration number in a three-crew configuration. In February 1998, Ansett began converting these five aircraft to the two-crew standard, which took roughly five days to complete for each airplane, except for one. VH-RMD did not have the dual electrical harnesses and was a hard-wired, three-crew aircraft and thus took substantially more hours to convert. It is noteworthy that the removal of the flight engineer's panel reduced the operational empty weight of each airplane by roughly 220 pounds.

Tex Boullioun had set the 757 certification target for December 1982, which involved a very fast-paced schedule

The Boeing 747-100 prototype (N7470, RA001, c/n 20235, l/n 1) was retained by Boeing for its entire career and was used as a test bed aircraft for the Rolls-Royce RB.211-535C engine that powered the first 757s. This aircraft currently is on display at the Museum of Flight in Seattle, Washington.
Courtesy of the Boeing Company

Courtesy of the Boeing Company via Chuck Ballard

for the team, particularly when much of Boeing's engineering resources were being used on the 767. Bill Robison, the 757 program's director of manufacturing, was concerned that the schedule was too compressed, since he hoped to have the certification slated for a later date in the summer of 1983. On the other hand, since Boullioun knew his team could do it, and that the schedule would make British Airways and Eastern happy, the target certification date remained.

ROLLOUT

On January 13, 1982, the first Boeing 757-200 (N757A) made its public debut. It was a magnificent sight, resplendent in its patriotic red, white, and blue paint scheme. The airplane rolled into the sunlight at the end of the 4-82 assembly hall at the Renton airport, celebrated by over 12,000 guests and employees. Tex Boullioun's wife, Jane, christened the airplane, stating, "To all the employees here at Boeing and to the employees at the supporting companies who made this a reality. May this great airplane, and the hundreds to follow, serve us well." T. Wilson had great confidence in the new airplane and was quoted as saying, "The 757 rollout marks the first public display of a new commercial jet transport which we think will become one of the most fuel-efficient aircraft ever built for the short-to-medium-range market."

The 757 prototype rolled out in Renton, Washington, amid much fanfare.
Courtesy of the Boeing Company

N757A is readied for flight testing. *Courtesy of the Boeing Company*

As was the Boeing tradition until the 777 program, the first flight pilots' names were painted below the cockpit windows prior to a prototype's first flight. This photo also gives a detailed view of the two pitot tubes and angle-of-attack vane. The silver circle is a static port used to collect flight test data and was not installed on production aircraft. *Courtesy of the Boeing Company*

757 FLIGHT TEST

About five weeks later, on February 19, 1982, N757A made its first flight under the excellent command of Capt. John Armstrong and Capt. Lew Wallick. The aircraft departed Renton under somewhat gusty wind conditions and reportedly had very nice handling qualities. The flight was not without a glitch, though, as Armstrong remembers: "What we did was to shut down an engine, and then we were going to relight it. We had a valve in there someplace that didn't open. Lew was over there trying to restart the engine. Finally, he did start to get it at about 500 feet on final approach, but I saw what was going on and just set up for a single-engine approach. We landed . . . and looked out and got a nice grease job, and everyone was happy. As I remember, it was a bleed valve that was supposed to supply air for the relight, and it wasn't opening."

When asked about the handling of the aircraft on the first flight, Capt. Armstrong continued: "It was great. It handled as planned, as with everything we had been doing in the simulator for several years. In fact, we came up with a beautiful control system on that airplane. It was a pilot's airplane . . . pilots really liked it. It was a narrow body, and you can tell the difference between a narrow body and a wide body. The 767 flew characteristically more like a 747, but the five-seven was pretty smooth, and we came up with a very nice control harmony there."

Flight testing for the 757 certification involved five aircraft. Ship 1 was considered a "prototype" aircraft and was retained by Boeing after certification. For the most part, the test program went smoothly, but as with any certification program, there were a few interesting moments and discoveries. One such event involved Ship 3, with Capt. Kenny Higgins at the controls. During the course of the flight, a transmission part in the drive system for the aircraft's high-lift devices seized, essentially making the wing flaps inoperative. This increased the safe approach speed for the aircraft to about 200 knots, nearly 60 knots faster

The 757 prototype lifts off on its maiden flight. *Courtesy of the Boeing Company*

LOAD LIMIT 1000 LBS

John Armstrong (*left*) and Lew Wallick emerge after the first flight of the 757-200. In an interview at the Museum of Flight, Capt. Wallick explained the sticker on his flight bag: "I decided that I trusted the ground crew. They knew their business, and there wasn't any point in thirty people standing around killing twenty minutes or thirty minutes while I looked at the airplane. So, I told the crew chiefs that on the airplanes that I was flying, I was going to kick the nosewheel tire, get on board, sign the papers, and leave, and if anything went wrong, I would come back and haunt them [*laughter*]. As a matter of fact, I think I got a better airplane that way.... They used to paint 'KICK HERE' on the nose tire on the 727 for me, so I knew exactly where to kick [*laughter*]. When we went over for the first flight of the 757, here was this decal on the nosewheel tire of the 757. I just took it off and put it on my flight bag, and that's how it ended up being in that photograph." This attitude won Wallick the respect and admiration of the entire flight test team. *Courtesy of the Boeing Company*

than normal. To make matters even more difficult, one of the components being tested was a new antiskid control system for the main wheel brakes. This unit was made by a different manufacturer than the original and possessed a hidden issue, about which no one was aware. There was an error associated with the programming of the component's computers, which sent incorrect signals to the airplane's braking system. So, when Higgins touched down, all four wheels on the right-side truck were completely locked to the point that none of the tires turned even a bit. All four wheels were ground down to the hub. While Higgins certainly knew something was wrong, he still tried to taxi clear of the runway—but no amount of engine power was going to make the airplane roll. Later, the problem with the control system was rectified, and even though the flap failure was not linked to the braking problem at all, the extra speed involved certainly was an additive factor. This

The starboard main landing gear touched down with all four wheels locked due to a malfunction in the aircraft's braking system. *Courtesy of the Boeing Company*

type of failure was considered to be a one-in-a-billion type of failure . . . nearly impossible.

Ship 3 went on to give Capt. Higgins another exciting experience. On November 16, 1982, the aircraft was being operated on a test flight fairly late into the program, with the 757 nearing certification. While flying above the northwest side of Mt. Rainier, they had a particularly severe encounter with icing over the Cascade Mountains. Jack Wimpress described the situation: "They got a real dose of it off the northwest side of Mt. Rainier. They iced up everything, including the engines, and the engines were making all kinds of strange noises and everything like that. Of course, they brought the airplane back as soon as they could. I looked at that fan, and every single one of the blades on that fan was damaged—every single one."

There was much speculation as to where the ice was coming from that had damaged both engines on Ship 3, since the inlet cowl was heated with hot engine bleed air and should not have allowed any ice to form ahead of the fan. There was even some conjecture that the engines were

A Boeing KC-135 with a specially installed spray boom could concentrate water, supercooled by flight at high altitudes, on specific portions of an aircraft flown in trail to evaluate ice formation and the effectiveness of the deicing/anti-icing systems. *Courtesy of the Boeing Company*

ingesting ice being shed from the nose, but Boeing needed to know the cause definitively and invent a solution quickly.

Boeing used a KC-135 tanker, retrofitted with a special boom that allowed water to be sprayed on another airplane flying behind it in close formation. With this setup being used during cold temperatures, the extreme icing conditions that damaged the engines of Ship 3 could be reproduced with water spray localized on different parts of the aircraft. It was soon found that the origin of the ice was from the engines' spinners, though it took a bit of doing to convince the folks at Rolls-Royce that this was indeed the problem. Rolls-Royce had tested the engine's intake design in wind tunnels, and since those tests showed that ice didn't form on the spinner at all, they saw no need to make provisions to heat the spinner. After some deliberation, the engineers from Rolls-Royce were convinced that there was indeed a spinner-icing problem, with further emphasis from the FAA representatives that they would not certify the engine unless the spinner was heated. Rolls-Royce's fix turned out to be quite simple, since the RB.211 had a hollow N1 (fan section) shaft leading up to the spinner. This was simply modified to carry hot engine bleed air up to the spinner dome to heat it, thereby solving the problem.

The Rolls-Royce RB.211-535C entered service with the heated-spinner modification, and this was the configuration used for its entire service life. It is noteworthy that the RB.211-535E4 used later on the 757 solved this problem by installing a rubber tip on the spinner. As the engine ran, this would vibrate and flex just enough to prevent ice formation in the spinner. Because of this, the later model of the engine did not require a heated spinner.

As an aside, during a gala held later to celebrate the 757 certification, there was a sizable gathering of Boeing employees, including the pilots, who were roasting each other in good fun. When Kenny Higgins came up on stage, he was presented with a T-shirt that read "Extremely Improbable," to which he retorted, "'Extremely improbable' to me means that it happened yesterday!"

FLUTTER

Aerodynamic flutter is a potentially dangerous phenomenon that can lead to structural failure of an aircraft if not properly damped out. Severe flutter occurs when an aircraft's wings or stabilizers flex up and down, becoming "divergent" with each cycle, essentially increasing in magnitude until the structural integrity of the aircraft is fatally compromised. Typically, aircraft become more susceptible to flutter at relatively high airspeeds and Mach numbers. To ensure that the 757 was indeed resistant to flutter, special vanes were attached to the wingtips and stabilizers; these vanes were designed to cause flutter to occur so the airframe's response could be determined. The 757 was found to be quite good in this regard and was naturally resistant to flutter.

Boeing used specially designed vanes to induce aerodynamic flutter on the wings and tail of this 757 flight test aircraft in March 1982. The 757 was found to be quite resistant to the onset of this potentially destructive phenomenon. *Courtesy of the Boeing Company*

High-speed taxi tests were conducted through a deep puddle of water to ascertain what portions of the aircraft would be affected by water deflected by the nose landing gear tires. The orange paint was water soluble and was washed off by the deflected water, making it clear where it struck the airframe. *Courtesy of the Boeing Company*

VMU TESTS

One of the more dramatic and important evaluations conducted on new jetliners during certification is known as Vmu (velocity, minimum unstick) testing, which was conducted with Ship 1 in June 1982. For the purposes of determining the minimum speed at which the aircraft can become airborne (or "unstuck," as it were), the test pilots conduct a takeoff in which they raise the nose of the aircraft much earlier, and to a higher angle, than normal. The test pilots do their best to gently set the aft fuselage on the runway while waiting for liftoff to occur. In order to protect the tail of the airplane, a specially fabricated oak skid was installed under the aft fuselage and sprayed with water to help keep it cool so as to prevent any possibility of a fire.

It is also important to note that another reason for Vmu testing goes back to the world's first commercial jetliner, the de Havilland Comet 1. The original wing design of this aircraft, combined with the anemic thrust output of its four Ghost engines, created a disastrous

The Vmu evaluation is conducted to establish the lowest possible liftoff speed for a given configuration, and also the aircraft's tolerance to abusive control inputs made by a pilot on takeoff. A special wooden tail skid was installed to protect the aft fuselage from damage. *Courtesy of the Boeing Company*

This oak tail skid was used to allow the aft fuselage to be intentionally set on the runway without causing damage to the aircraft. *Courtesy of the Boeing Company via Duane Jackson*

The cabin doors on the 757 were substantially heavier than those of the other Boeing narrow-bodied aircraft, mainly due to the larger slide required by the aircraft's tall stance on the ramp. *Courtesy of the Boeing Company*

situation if the pilot raised the nose too early on takeoff. The wing, instead of providing the necessary lift to fly, would merely plow its way through the passing air, thereby causing so much induced drag that the aircraft would simply stop accelerating and careen off the end of the runway. Vmu testing is therefore used to confirm that the airplane will still fly and climb out after an early or abusive nose-up control input during takeoff.

DOOR ISSUES

The 757 was different from the legacy Boeing narrow bodies in that it sat much higher off the ground. Emergency egress via inflatable slides had been industry standard for decades, and the 757 was going to follow suit. Due to the airplane's high stance, combined with the slides needing to be usable in any landing gear configuration, (e.g., a rear slide deployed with a collapsed nose gear), the slides on the 757 were quite a bit larger than those on the 707/727/737. This, in turn, caused a major redesign of the cabin doors, which increased the weight of each to 323 pounds.

Eastern Airlines sent operations agent Nancy Ballard out to evaluate the opening and closing of the doors. She was fairly small in stature, at 115 pounds, and found opening the door extremely difficult. It was subsequently measured that 70 pounds of force was required to open the exit, which was unacceptable both operationally and especially for emergency egress situations. Since this discovery occurred in the eleventh hour, it required an immediate remedy. The engineers went back to their drawing boards to find a solution, and eight weeks later, just prior to FAA certification, the hard-working Boeing engineers produced the solution. A dual-spring assembly

An emergency egress slide is seen deployed from the L1 exit. The large size of the slide is apparent in the photo. *Courtesy of the Boeing Company*

The wings of the 757 structural test article are bent upward, using hydraulic jacks to establish the ultimate strength of the structure. *Courtesy of the Boeing Company*

was installed to make the handling loads of the heavy 757 door significantly less, also illustrating once again how the airline's input that Boeing invited helped turn out a superior product.

757 STRUCTURAL TESTING

For every new aircraft type that Boeing designs, they build an airframe that is never intended to leave the ground. This test rig is used to simulate multiple flight cycles by imposing flight loads on the structure with hydraulic jacks. Engineers monitor the airframe, looking for any place that may suffer from metal fatigue or inadequate static strength. After finishing this "operational" simulation, the test airframe is then stressed to destruction to assess the aircraft's absolute strength. On July 16, 1982, the test airframe had such high loads imposed on the wings that they bent upward 11 feet, 6 inches, before breaking with a thunderous bang. When the calculations were reviewed, the 757 airframe was shown to be 12% stronger than estimated.

GLOBAL SALES TOURS

Boeing conducted sales tours with N505EA (c/n 22195, l/n 6), which included visits to airline customers in Africa, Europe, the Middle East, and the Americas during October and November 1982. In addition to showing the world the new jet, the tours also provided operational-reliability data for FAA certification. On one such tour, N505EA flew sixty-seven flights totaling 46,660 nautical miles, with stops in sixteen different countries, without a single mechanical delay. This was a testament to the robust reliability of the 757 design.

The test program encompassed 1,380 hours of flight, putting the new jet through conditions designed to exceed those likely to be experienced under normal airline operations. In many aspects, the 757 performed even better

Ship 6 is seen in Manila, Philippines, during one of the 757 sales tours. *Courtesy of the Boeing Company*

Inside the aircraft, temporary marketing displays were installed to highlight the features of the 757 to potential airline customers. *Courtesy of the Boeing Company*

Ship 6 rests in Stockholm, Sweden, as representatives from Scandinavian Airlines (SAS) tour the airplane. *Courtesy of the Boeing Company*

During Ship 6's visit to England, it flew in formation with a Griffon-powered Supermarine Spitfire F.XIVc (RM 689/AP-D, c/n 6S/432263). While this was an amazing display with two beautiful aircraft, further significance is that both machines were Rolls-Royce powered. Sadly, RM 689 was lost during the Woodford Air Show in 1992. *Courtesy of the Boeing Company*

London's Heathrow Airport was an important stop for the 757, since British Airways was one of the its launch customers. The British national carrier was a longtime Boeing customer, dating back to the Boeing 377 Stratocruiser. The Boeing 707-336B seen in the background (G-AXXZ, c/n 20457, l/n 853) was delivered to the carrier in 1971 and was subsequently damaged beyond repair during a rejected takeoff while being operated by the Benin government as TY-BBR in 1985. *Courtesy of the Boeing Company*

A Boeing test pilot, Captain Brien Wygle, occupies the left seat during a 757 demonstration flight. Known to be kind and friendly, Capt. Wygle was also regarded by those who worked with him as an exceptionally gifted aviator. *Courtesy of the Boeing Company*

During another sales tour, the 757 is brought into the rural airport at Chengdu, China. The pilot in the right seat has his hand on the flap lever, indicating that he is ready in case a go-around is required. *Courtesy of the Boeing Company*

Ship 6 visited Rome to display the 757 for Alitalia. The Italian carrier was operating a fleet of 727-200s, making them a logical customer for the 757. While the airline never purchased the 757, they later utilized the larger 767-300. *Courtesy of the Boeing Company*

Lew Wallick is seen in a 757 with Dean Melton, FAA chief of flight test branch, in the captain's seat prior to a test flight. *Courtesy of the Boeing Company*

than anticipated. Wing efficiency when compared to that of the 727 was estimated to be improved by 12%, but flight testing proved it to be nearly 17% better. The 757 also had a wide center-of-gravity envelope, which was tested from 9% to 39% of mean aerodynamic chord (MAC), allowing significant flexibility when loading passengers and cargo.

The 757 demonstrated a fuel savings of 3.1% to 4.6% for the actual aircraft over engineering estimates too. Aside from the efficiencies generated by the wing, Boeing had spent extra effort to build the highest-quality aircraft possible, so in areas where the fuselage's skins overlapped, protruding rivets, seal leaks, and antennae were all minimized, adding to the 757's incredible efficiency. The fuselage's semimonocoque structure was made of 2024 and 7075 aluminum alloys for excellent strength and weight characteristics too.

Braking performance was also exceptionally good, thanks to the new carbon fiber brakes, using 250 feet less

runway on average to come to a complete stop as compared to the engineering calculations. One such extreme set of evaluations were called Vmbe (Velocity, maximum brake energy) tests, during which the aircraft was taken up to flying speed at maximum weight before performing a rejected takeoff (RTO). The brakes on the 757 were incredibly effective and performed quite well.

The author was a deadheading pilot aboard a Delta Air Lines flight, departing Atlanta for Miami when, at 110 knots (just prior to decision speed), the captain rejected the takeoff for a mechanical issue. I was amazed that the airplane was virtually stopped before the engines could even fully accelerate in reverse thrust. Even though I have experienced this in the simulator many times in other aircraft types, they were nothing compared to a real-life V1 abort, and the nearly violent level of braking required to safely stop the airplane.

Ship 1 is seen during rejected takeoff (RTO) trials. An RTO is one of the most abusive maneuvers that aircraft have to be able to perform during testing. For this, the aircraft is typically loaded to maximum takeoff weight, accelerated to takeoff decision speed (V1), and suddenly stopped by using maximum braking and no reverse thrust. As seen in the photo, the sheer kinetic energy absorbed by the brakes is extremely high, generating a significant amount of heat. The airplane must be able to withstand the hot-brake situation for at least five minutes prior to the arrival of airport fire personnel. *Courtesy of the Boeing Company*

On December 21, 1982, the Boeing 757-200 received its type certificate from the Federal Aviation Administration. Boeing's 757 technology manager, Bob Davis, wrote the following in his work titled *The Development and Certification of the Boeing 757*, which was prepared for the Canadian Aeronautics and Space Institute Symposium in April 1984: "Flight test had prepared itself with improved data acquisition systems to be in a position to support two new airplanes with overlapping schedules. This meant acquiring and handling more data than any previous period of time. The combined effort of the engineering design team and the flight test department played a major role in certifying the 757 airplane two days ahead of the schedule that had been established four years earlier."

THE B757 INITIAL TYPE CERTIFICATION "JUMP SEAT SAGA" WITH CAPTAIN TOM IMRICH

This is the little-known story of a "side event" that occurred during the B757's original FAA type certification (TC), which ended up playing a significant role in modern jet transport flight deck design, air carrier operations, authority regulation, and flight crew complement.

A "jump seat" is a flight deck seat placed near or between the pilot seats of modern air transport jets, for use by FAA inspectors performing pilot or airline qualification checks, or airline check airmen monitoring flight crew performance, routes, facilities, airports, or procedures. It also serves for new pilot upgrades as part of initial operating experience (IOE), or now known simply as operating experience (OE).

During the original FAA type certification (TC) of the B757 in 1982, the airlines, authorities, labor organizations, and OEMs were in the last vestiges of a heated battle on the backside of a contentious controversy regarding the "two-man crew" vs. "three-man crew" complement. The Presidential Task Force was led by former FAA administrator John McLucas. Largely at the urging of some airline customers, to preclude a jump seat occupant from ever again becoming a required part of the flight crew, as well as for reasons of efficiency of the flight deck design space, the original B757 jump seat was placed in a low and outboard position in the flight deck. There, an occupant of the jump seat could see little of the flight instruments, displays, controls, or relevant critical outside view (e.g., runways, taxiways, and other airborne traffic). The jump seat occupant could certainly not reach any cockpit controls or switches or easily communicate with the other pilots.

The relevant history of crew duties assigned to a jump seat occupant happened early on the B737, with the jump seat supernumerary serving as a third crew member at some airlines. So, this jump seat issue drew the direct attention of industry leadership, up to at least the FAA administrator J. Lynn Helms and EAL president Frank Borman, among other airline top executives. Others involved were senior Boeing leadership, along with industry and pilot labor organizations including ATA and ALPA.

The Approved 757 Jumpseat

Courtesy of Thomas Imrich Jr.

UNDERSTANDING THE REGULATIONS

Aircraft are designed, built, and flown in strict accordance with regulations. Many of these were written given past experiences and accident histories, ensuring that safety is always held high and that the industry, as a whole, strives to be safer every day. The Federal Aviation Administration governed the initial certification of the 757, and thus its regulations are paramount in this account. It is important to know that foreign counties have their own regulations, which a new American-built airplane such as the 757 must be shown in compliance with prior to being operated with their respective national airlines.

Author's note: A quick review of the FAA regulations in play during this jump seat challenge is important for understanding. Here is a description of the relevant federal aviation regulations (FAR):

- FAR Part 25 pertains to the certification of air carrier aircraft. This is inclusive of all jetliners and certain large turboprop aircraft that serve in airline service. This regulation superseded CAR 4b and required more-stringent standards in many aspects, especially with regard to cockpit design and human factors.
- FAR 121 governs air carrier operations in general.
- FAR 121.581 pertains to cockpit observation access and states:
  (a) Each certificate holder shall make available a seat on the flight deck of each airplane, used by it in air commerce, for occupancy by the Administrator while conducting en route inspections. The location and equipment of the seat, with respect to its suitability for use in conducting en route inspections, is determined by the Administrator.
  (b) In each airplane that has more than one observer's seat, in addition to the seats required for the crew complement for which the airplane was certificated, the forward observer's seat or the observer's seat selected by the Administrator must be made available when complying with paragraph (a) of this section.
- FAR 91 pertains to operating rules that are more basic in nature, governing aviation in general. Airspace rules and general operating requirements are a good example of this blanket set of regulations, which also pertain to general aviation.
- FAR 61 pertains to basic pilot qualifications for ratings, including the Airline Transport Pilot (ATP) rating.

The Boeing-proposed aft, low, and outboard jump seat position for the 757 inhibited the ability of any Authority inspector, check airman, or observing pilot to effectively perform regulatory specified and essential functions or duties (e.g., FAA air carrier ops inspectors, airline line check airman, or pilots fulfilling IOE requirements). Further, there were also significant complaints from authorities and airlines alike to FAA field offices about the functional inadequacy and position of the B767 jump seat, for which the B767 had already been FAR 25 type-certificated back in July 1982 and had already entered FAR 121 airline service.

Boeing had been advised many months ahead of time by FAA Flight Standards (the FAA's Transport "Aircraft Evaluation Group" [AEG]), long before B757 TC, that the B757 jump seat was considered by FAA to likely be unacceptable, and determined to not be in compliance with CFR14 Part 121.581.

This noncompliance issue persisted unresolved and contentious for months, with "back-and-forth" communications among the FAA Transport AEG, the FAA Seattle Aircraft Certification Office (SACO), FAA Washington Headquarters, and Boeing. Some communications could have been characterized as the FAA implying that the B757 FAR 25 TC was being put at risk, or alternately, Boeing was considered by the FAA to be "stonewalling" any change needed for providing a rule-compliant jump seat. Boeing contended that the jump seat issue was an airline operations problem that needed to be addressed later, and solved by the airlines, so it did not require Boeing responding or initiating a design change prior to TC issuance. Boeing asserted that since it was a FAR 121 rule being questioned, the matter didn't, and shouldn't, affect Boeing's FAR 25 TC.

This assertion was later confirmed to be incorrect—which is why the FAA type inspection authorization (TIA) item 18c now exists: to explicitly ensure that in any FAR 25 transport aircraft certification, FAA Operating Rule potential compliance can be met (e.g., FAR 121, 91, and 61). TIA item 18c ensures that Operations Rule "Pre-coordination" occurs, with an FAA Operations agreement that's necessary for any FAR 25 TC action, prior to FAR 25 TC issuance. Without successful Operations (Flight Standards) coordination and agreement, an FAR 25 TC cannot be completed, and a Part 25 type certificate cannot therefore be issued.

Boeing did make a few attempts at several token proposed mockup changes for the jump seat, with some FAA assessment exercises along the way. However, none of these changes came close to solving the issue or achieving FAA agreement that the changes satisfied the FAR 121.581 rule requirement. The FAA-Boeing standoff, which the airlines closely watched from the background, continued to be unresolved right up until the scheduled B757 original type certification day, on December 21, 1982.

That was a day I will never forget. There was much more at stake here than simply the B757's inappropriate and non-compliant jump seat position. Instead, it was also a principle being challenged: that it was acceptable to issue an FAR 25 type certificate for an air carrier aircraft known to be non-compliant with a key, applicable, and necessary operating rule (in this case, FAR 121.581).

With precoordination all the way up to and including the FAA administrator (J. Lynn Helms) and the lead Region for Transport Aircraft and FAA region director (Chuck Foster), I drew the "short straw." I was the FAA representative nominated by the region director, as the responsible FAA Transport AEG chief, to go to Boeing in person and deliver the bad news one to one from the FAA directly, to the Boeing vice president in charge of the B757. The message was that "FAA does not intend to and will not FAR 25 certificate the B757, until and unless the jump seat design is modified and found acceptable to the FAA." As I remember it, the dead silence before what I expected as an eventual explosion perhaps lasted a whole ten seconds.

That was not a happy day in Renton. All the aviation press members were already assembled outside the Boeing VP's office, ready for the major press releases and a major celebration to follow, since I was officially informing Boeing from the FAA that there would be no B757 type certificate issued until and unless the jump seat was modified. The language of that afternoon was most "colorful," to say the least. An absolute flurry of phone calls between the FAA and Boeing followed, both within Boeing and the FAA too. Even lawsuits were threatened.

But after it all, and only a few hours later, a pathway forward was informally negotiated, defined, and agreed to by both the FAA and Boeing. The proposal was to salvage the moment by still issuing a B757 TC that day, but the TC would instead be only a temporary expiring "provisional B757 TC." It would be conditioned on Boeing fully implementing an acceptable jump seat design that satisfied all FAA FAR requirements. At FAA's insistence, the provisional B757 TC would expire by a near-term deadline, if the revised jump seat design and installations, in all B757s built to that point and planned afterward, didn't fully meet with FAA rule compliance, before the provisional B757 TC's expiration date.

The jump seat modifications would need to be reviewed by and found acceptable to a newly defined high-level FAA Headquarters Flight Standards special review team. With that agreement by Boeing, a provisional FAR 25 type certificate was issued by the FAA on that same day, December 21, 1982. The proposed "provisional" B757 TC was worded to expire by the following June if a newly designed jump seat was not subsequently found to be adequate and acceptable to the FAA. The review team making that FAA jump seat re-design determination would personally be headed up by the FAA's director of flight operations (AFO-1) from the FAA's Washington (DC) headquarters. Additional specific criteria for the seat's acceptability were also to be defined and provided to Boeing, to more clearly identify the needed jump seat changes.

Further, as a result of FAA field office complaints already received about the B767's jump seat, and a pending lawsuit by Boeing against the FAA over the jump seat issue, the FAA initiated a draft AD action against the B767 jump seat's design in April 1983. Boeing eventually also agreed to fix the B767 jump seat installation, too, consistent with the newly established criteria, albeit with grandfather rights afforded by FAA to Boeing to be able to retain the jump seat configuration for the small number of B767s already manufactured and delivered to customers, many of which were already in service.

New and more-comprehensive criteria for compliance with FAR 121.581 were also developed by the FAA, and a new, re-positioned jump seat location for the B757 was proposed by Boeing. The AFO-1 review team assessed that design and accepted the adequacy of the modified seat position as fully complying with CFR 14 Part 121.581 (see pictures of the B757 current jump seat installation). Production B757s were subsequently modified prior to delivery, and before the B757 provisional TC's expiration. An unrestricted B757 type certificate was issued after the revised jump seat design was accepted by FAA, and after affected B757 aircraft in production were appropriately modified.

It's noteworthy that the airlines had such concern over the potential for the issue not being successfully resolved between Boeing and the FAA, and that at least the initial operator, Eastern Airlines, actually applied for and was granted an FAA exemption to allow the airline to fly the provisionally certificated B757 with use of the noncompliant seat until they had a fully compliant jump seat installed.

The upshot of this story was that a vital principle was upheld: that an air transport aircraft intended for airline service will not be allowed to be type-certificated by FAA under provisions of FAR 25 if it cannot also be shown to be capable of legally and safely being used and flown under the relevant operating rules (e.g., FAR 121, 91, 61). The critical role, function, and requirements for meaningful jump seat access for Authority Operations inspections (e.g., FAA) and flight crew, procedures, and facilities assessment (e.g., by airline check airmen) were upheld, including for pilot crew members completing initial operating experience (IOE).

Finally, the repositioned jump seats for the B767 later played a key role for airlines to facilitate the use of augmented crew members for operating long-range, long-duration flights. Many B767 flights eventually needed to operate well over eight hours of flight time. For those long-range operations, an additional third pilot was typically needed as part of the flight crew anyway, to satisfy flight and duty time requirements (e.g., during the evolving ETOPS long-range-flight era).

And that's the amazing, little-known story of the B757 initial FAR 25 type certification, and the outsized role the B757's jump seat played. To this day, it underscores the important relationship between FAR 25—and necessary parallel potential rule compliance with FAR 121—and all relevant operating rules!

INTO SERVICE

Boeing and Eastern Airlines wasted no time in getting the 757 into service. On December 22, 1982, Eastern took delivery of N506EA (c/n 22196, l/n 7) and put it into revenue service less than two weeks later, on January 1, 1983. Frank Borman, a man not easily impressed, was very happy with his new jet, reportedly even saying that the production aircraft that he was operating was enormously better than the airplane he had bought back in 1978. This airplane was going to be a winner.

The 757 went through a metamorphosis of sorts after being purchased by British Airways. This model shows the change from a T-tail to a conventional tail but still sports the 727/737-style cockpit profile. *Courtesy of the Boeing Company*

The changing of the guard: Ship 2 (N501EA, c/n 22191, l/n 2) rests next to two brand-new 727-225s prior to their delivery to the airline. For many airlines, the 757 effectively replaced the 727 just as the designers had originally intended. *Courtesy of the Boeing Company*

THE BRITISH AIRWAYS DELIVERY

Trailing the FAA certification by a few weeks, G-BIKA (c/n 22172, l/n 9) was used to complete British CAA certification. This was accomplished on January 14, 1983, with a celebration of the first aircraft delivery. This aircraft (G-BIKB, c/n22173, l/n 10) was christened *Windsor Castle*, since it was traditional for British Airways to name each 757 after one of the island nation's many castles. She was accompanied in the ceremony by *Edinburgh Castle* (G-BIKC, c/n 22174, l/n 11), which was the next to be delivered on January 31, 1983.

G-BIKA is seen during a predelivery test flight prior to spending seventeen years in service with the carrier. This airplane was converted to a 757-200F in July 2000 and flew with DHL before being scrapped in late 2017. *Courtesy of the Boeing Company*

Lord King of British Airways looks at the camera as T. Wilson signs the papers for the first 757 delivery to the English carrier. *Courtesy of the Boeing Company*

Courtesy of the Boeing Company

ESTABLISHING THE FIRST BOEING "B757 B767" FAA PILOT "COMMON TYPE RATING"

The 757 and 767 emerged from this transformative period of jet transport evolution with the exploratory idea of a common pilot type rating that would allow pilots qualified and type-rated in one model to be authorized to fly the other. For these two airplanes, one narrow bodied and one wide bodied with separate type certificates, this was quite different from the "same" pilot type rating encompassing more than one version of a single airplane type, such as the 737-100 and 737-200. I am pleased to provide a sidebar on this important subject, authored by two people who were on the scene at the time: 757 Flight Deck Project engineer Peter Morton, and the FAA Aircraft Evaluation Group (AEG) leader, Captain Tom Imrich.

BOEING FLIGHT DECK LEAD PETER MORTON

I joined the 757 program at the end of 1978, when the airplane configuration was becoming firm; probably a bit later for a major derivative of the 727 than was comfortable for the cost and schedule folks. There was little or no similarity to the 767, which by then was formally launched and was a three-crew conventional tail configuration, with cockpit geometry unlike any previous Boeing airplane. I remember a conversation with my boss, Phil Condit, wondering, "Wouldn't it be amazing if we could have a common-enough design with the 767 so a pilot qualified in one was qualified in the other!" I knew the 767 launch customers had all signed up for a three-crew configuration in exchange for labor peace with ALPA, but I also knew that Pacific Western, a Canadian airline that I'd worked with on their 737 introduction, was going to acquire the 767, and they would insist on a two-crew flight deck. I had a strange background for the job; our preeminent flight deck design leader was Harty Stoll, already assigned to the 767 program, and it was clear that the folks who would populate 757 engineering would be stretched

This was a rare photo opportunity, with the 767 and 757 prototypes parked nose to nose with Capt. Lew Wallick in the foreground with a restored Boeing 100, a commercial version of the Boeing F4B-1 Navy fighter. Naturally, the 757 and 767 shared cockpit and systems commonality, but they also had much in common with Boeing's early aircraft. Unlike some other manufacturers, Boeing's philosophy remains that the pilot should have full and complete control of the aircraft, regardless of the state-of-the art systems involved. *Courtesy of the Boeing Company*

for resources. It was kind of unusual that Phil would pick a marketing and training guy to take responsibility for the 757 flight deck. Yes, I was an engineer by education, but because I had been in marketing so long, Phil's then boss Jim Copenhaver affectionately called me "Yellow Pages" in reference to my persistence as 737 marketing manager to argue for more features and more capability so we could outwit the Douglas competition in sales campaigns. My advocacy for a common pilot type rating was an outgrowth of understanding airline economics, and how powerful a sales tactic it would be to show airlines a fleet that would go from 180 to 350 passengers with the same flight crew; no extra expenses for pilot training and currency maintenance . . . what a dream!

Of course, we wanted EFIS on the 757, and the 767 had it developed and ready to plug and play, except those long cathode ray tubes would not fit in the 737 cockpit geometry without modifying structure that hearkened back to the 707 and KC-135. This problem went away when an idea of mating the wide-body 767 flight deck with the narrow-body 757 fuselage structure gained traction. And, once the 757 program had been launched and our T-tail had become a conventional back end, the 757 and 767 began to "look alike," and the idea of common pilot duties grew more plausible.

It would be 1981 (two years later) before the issue of crew complement, obviously a big part of the puzzle, would be cemented in stone. After Jim Copenhaver retired, Phil Condit became director of engineering, and he was committed to protecting the common-pilot option. Phil, Everette Webb, his counterpart on the 767, and Ken Holtby sat down with a number of program stakeholders, including sales and marketing, and concluded that the emergent idea of a common pilot type rating for the two airplanes was worth addressing as a formal engineering objective. Because there were fundamental differences in the 757 and 767 systems, left to normal processes, they would have manifested as a multitude of significant differences in controls and indicators, and the way airplane systems had to be managed. Examples included the leading and trailing edge flap schedules in response to the flap lever control being different, along with different flap angles for corresponding phases of flight. Hydraulic pumps on the 767 were bleed air driven, with more capacity to move the larger landing gear too. Aileron control wheels on the 767 used a geared torque tube to move the aileron cables and had a maximum throw of about 78 degrees, while the 757 aileron control was a system reminiscent of the 707/727/737, with about 115 degrees of throw either side of neutral. The list went on and on.

Ken decided to form a Flight Deck Design Committee (FDDC), whose mission was to identify all significant differences in the airplanes, determine if they were an impediment to a common pilot rating, and, if necessary, recommend changes to either the 757 or 767 to resolve the issue. Every change to protect an as-yet-still-ephemeral common pilot type rating would put the affected program and its leaders under additional cost and schedule stress. Ken rightly realized that he should be the arbiter, because as the senior engineering authority in Boeing Commercial, both programs reported to him.

Del Fadden, chief engineer of Flight Deck staff for both programs, was tapped to lead the FDDC. This was a "night job" for Del, while he retained his duties serving both programs. He called a meeting every week and populated his committee with the two Flight Deck senior project engineers (Harty Stoll and me); the project pilots John Armstrong, Kenny Higgins, and Tom Edmonds; training pilots as consultants; and, frankly, anyone else he needed to address and resolve issues. Our meetings were long and painstaking; one time an engineering leader, John Winch, from elsewhere in the company, was called on to audit the FDDC activity, and after sitting through one meeting, he muttered, "You guys argue for three hours about the function of a single alternate-action push-button switch; that's enough for me!" Satisfied we were doing a thorough job, John retreated back to his job in Boeing Military.

Slowly, the airplanes converged from a pilot-operational perspective. In one case, Del's psychology expert, Frank Ruggiero, did human-factors research in a special cockpit mockup to determine the subjective significance of the aileron wheel throw differences. In another action item, the stability and control aerodynamics staff submitted a detailed analysis of roll and pitch rate differences between the airplanes and determined that the resulting maneuver characteristics were within a range of commonly experienced variation arising from weight and center-of-gravity changes on a typical aircraft. In some cases, a design change was necessary, and the dreaded formal authorization called a

PRR (Production Revision Request) would be released to physically modify the airplane.

After the July 1981 determination by a presidential task force that two-crew was as safe as three-crew, and the request from 767 launch customers to convert their airplanes to two-crew, Boeing invited senior flight operations representatives of American, United, TWA, and Delta to Seattle and presented the 757 flight deck to them as the most expedient pathway that might be feasible, while preserving, as close as possible, their contract delivery schedules. They were asked to all agree on the same flight deck configuration with no customization or unique features, which they did—a highly unusual agreement, considering traditions of airline independence in configuring their airplanes.

The hero of what ensued was Clifford Coomes, an iconic leader in factory operations. Cliff was a colorful, outspoken character; asked if he could expeditiously modify the three-crew 767s, he said, in effect, "Give me a site away from the factory, let me pick my team, and leave me alone. I can make it happen!" The fifth three-crew 767 airplane had completed systems functional tests in the factory; it was towed to a remote hangar at Everett, and in about thirty days it rolled back out ready to fly with the first 767 two-crew flight deck. The airplane served as the test platform to certify crew workload and completed its other function and reliability testing, and the 767 received its airplane type certificate on schedule. There were many ship sets of three-crew 767 parts in the supply pipeline; Cliff's team repeated the process about thirty times before the production line began to produce "native" two-crew airplanes, with none, to my memory, being delivered late.

The stage was now truly set for the common pilot type rating. When Delta ordered 757s, it became the first operator with both types in its fleet, and Boeing worked with the FAA to design a means of confirming that the concept was safe, procedurally compliant with crew certification rules, and practical operationally. This story is best told by Capt. Tom Imrich, who both was involved in the aircraft type certifications and led the Flight Standardization Board associated with crew qualifications. Capt. Imrich, the FAA's Transport Aircraft Evaluation Group chief, gives the administrator's perspective:

Using the "same" pilot type rating for derivative aircraft types, or using a "common" pilot type rating for different aircraft types, as designated on an FAA airline transport pilot's license, dates back to decades before the advent of the B757 and B767. However, the "same" or "common" license designations typically applied only to very similar derivative or related models, such as the Convair 240/340/440 or, later in the jet age, to the Boeing 707 and Boeing 720. In fact, it was even thought to be a stretch for FAA to extend the B707/ B720 pilot type rating to cover the military C-135, a version of a jet that had similarity to the B707 in external shape, size, form, handling, and performance but had a very different flight deck. However numerous military aviators sought credit

Capt. Thomas Imrich's career included being a technical pilot for the United States Air Force and then later for the Federal Aviation Administration, where he worked to certify the common type rating for the 757 and 767. Capt. Imrich eventually flew for Boeing Flight Test and was selected as a First Flight pilot on the Boeing 747-8. *Courtesy of Capt. Thomas Imrich*

for having qualified as a PIC in military service in the C-135 or KC-135, and FAA believed at the time the similarities of these different aircraft types were adequate to allow those military pilots to still qualify for receiving a "B707/B720" type rating on the basis of their military experience in the C-135.

In the early 1980s, the significant difference with introducing the requested "common type rating" for pilots of the B757 and B767 was that these types were two very different aircraft. The B757 and B767 were certificated on two entirely different aircraft type certificates, one was a single aisle and the other a wide body, they had quite different physical geometry, they had different models of engines, they had different pilot "eye heights" when landing, and they had significant systems differences. The question of the day for Boeing and the FAA was if they could be made sufficiently common from a pilot's perspective, with similar controls, handling characteristics, instrument displays, aircraft systems use, and normal and non-normal operating procedures, so that a common FAA type qualification could be used for pilots. That, it was hoped, would allow for the pilots to hold the same qualification rating on their pilot's certificate for both. A pilot qualifying to fly a B767 would then also be considered as FAA type-rated to fly a B757, and vice versa. It would also allow for pilots to be more readily assigned to flying both types at an airline, in a mixed fleet of B757s and B767s.

The FAA first received formal word of Boeing's interest in pursuing this common pilot qualification goal shortly prior to November 26, 1979. That's when I was first appointed as the chairman of the Joint B757 B767 Flight Standardization Board, as it was initially established. From that point, work progressed inside Boeing in an attempt to make the two aircraft types' flight decks, handling characteristics, crew procedures, and outside view vision polar, as similar as possible. Significant coordination was needed between the FAA and industry, as well as with Boeing, where the topic was still contested and finally "put to bed" as a major industry controversy over the "two-man crew" versus "three-man crew" issue with the McLucas "Presidential Commission" in mid-1981.

The B767 was type-certificated on July 30, 1982. Then, on August 27, 1982, Boeing formally applied to FAA requesting that FAA consider issuing a common type rating for the B757 and B767, even though the B757 was not to be certificated until December 1982. By early 1983, Boeing and FAA had generally agreed on a methodology to use in making the "common type rating" determination. It was agreed that Boeing would produce a "commonality document" illustrating similarities and differences between the two types, then do simulator tests with pilot test subjects and validate those simulator tests with real aircraft test flights. The tests even included cases of the subject pilots demonstrating they could safely fly the other type without having had previous training on that type, even when using the inappropriate checklist for that type. After all the simulator assessments, a flight validation would be conducted using real aircraft. Actual flight demonstrations by the subject pilots would be required, showing that after those pilots received training only in their "base" aircraft, either a B757 or B767, they could then safely and proficiently fly all the "regulatory required" flight test maneuvers for the pilot type rating in the other aircraft type, for which they had no prior training in that specific model.

Within the FAA, there was by no means broad agreement of the suitability, or even the legality, of issuing such a pilot "common type rating" for two apparently significantly different aircraft types. Getting convergence and agreement inside the FAA was nothing short of a herculean task, not to mention addressing vocal opposition from some nonparticipating OEMs, airlines, and pilot groups. Even the criteria to be applied by the FAA for the testing was still controversial until just a few days before the final decision was made. However, in the end, the Boeing designs for the B757 and B767, as well as test preparation and testing results, were all consistent with meeting the agreed-on criteria.

So, while serving as the FAA Transport Aircraft Evaluation Group chief, and having been designated by the FAA as the FAA chairman for the joint "B757/B767 Flight Standardization Board," on that infamous day of July 19, 1983, I signed the

NORMAL **757/767** CHECKLISTS

BEFORE START CHECKLIST

CHALLENGE (F)	RESPONSE
DEPARTURE BRIEFING	COMPLETE (C)
FMCs, RADIOS	PROGRAMMED, SET FOR DEPARTURE (C, F)
IRS	NAV, ALIGNED (C)
FUEL PANEL	PUMPS ON, CROSSFEED CLOSED (C)
FUEL QUANTITY	POUNDS, CLEARED WITH _____ POUNDS (C)
CABIN SIGNS	ON (C)
HYDRAULIC QUANTITY	NORMAL (C)
OXYGEN CHECK	COMPLETE (C, F)
OIL QUANTITY	NORMAL (C)
AUTOBRAKES	RTO (C)
PARKING BRAKE	SET, PRESSURE NORMAL (C, F)
ALTIMETERS	SET (C, F) (In hPa)
AIRSPEED BUGS	GW ____ FLAPS ____ SET (C, F) (V1) (Vr) (V2)
FUEL CONTROL SWITCHES	CUTOFF (C)
TRIM	SET (C)

BEFORE PUSHBACK CHECKLIST

CHALLENGE (F)	RESPONSE
SLIDING WINDOWS	CLOSED AND LOCKED (C, F)
DOORS	CLOSED (C)
CABIN PREPARATION	COMPLETE (C)

BEFORE TAKEOFF CHECKLIST

CHALLENGE (F)	RESPONSE
FLAPS	PLANNED, ____ INDICATED, DETENT (C)
CONTROL CHECK	COMPLETE (C, F)
ENGINE ANTI-ICE	ON/OFF (C)
ISOLATION SWITCHES	(757) OFF / (767) LEFT AND RIGHT OFF (F)
FUEL CONTROL SWITCHES	RUN, LOCKED (C)

MANIFEST CHANGES

TRIM, WEIGHT, SPEEDS	CHECKED (F), SET (C, F)
FMCs, RADIOS	PROGRAMMED, SET FOR DEPARTURE (C, F)
THRUST	REDUCED/MAX EPR, SET (C)
MCP	V2 ____, HEADING ____, ALTITUDE ____, SET (C)

FINAL ITEMS

CABIN NOTIFICATION	COMPLETE (F)
AUTOTHROTTLE	ARMED (F)
TRANSPONDER	ON/TA-RA (F)
EICAS	RECALLED, CANCELLED (F)

12/6/83   FAA APPROVED   9F14032-9

AFTER TAKEOFF CHECKLIST
(To be checked ALOUD by the pilot not flying)

| LANDING GEAR LEVER | OFF |
| FLAPS | UP |

APPROACH DESCENT CHECKLIST
(To be checked ALOUD by the pilot not flying)

APPROACH BRIEFING	COMPLETE
FMCs, RADIOS	PROGRAMMED, SET FOR APPROACH
EICAS	RECALLED, CANCELLED
LANDING ALTITUDE	SET
AIRSPEED BUGS	GW ____ FLAPS ____ SET (REF)

TRANSITION LEVEL

| AUTOBRAKES | LEVEL ____ OFF |
| ALTIMETERS | SET (In hPa) |

FINAL DESCENT CHECKLIST
(To be checked ALOUD by the pilot not flying)

CABIN NOTIFICATION	COMPLETE
LANDING GEAR	DOWN, 3 GREEN LIGHTS
SPEED BRAKES	ARMED
FLAPS	PLANNED, ____ INDICATED

PARKING CHECKLIST

CHALLENGE (F)	RESPONSE
PARKING BRAKE	SET, PRESSURE NORMAL (C)
FUEL CONTROL SWITCHES	CUT OFF, FUEL FLOW ZERO (C)
AUTOTHROTTLE	OFF (C)
HYDRAULIC PUMPS	OFF, EXCEPT ENGINES (C)
ANTI-ICE	OFF (C)
FUEL PUMPS	OFF (C)
ENGINE START SELECTORS	OFF (C)
EMERGENCY EXIT LIGHTS	OFF (C)
CARGO HEAT (767)	OFF (C)
WINDOW HEAT	OFF (C)
EQUIPMENT COOLING (767)	AUTO/REFRIG (C)
RADAR	OFF (C)
TRANSPONDER	STANDBY (C)
IRS	OFF (C)

REFER TO THE NORMAL PROCEDURES CHAPTER TO SECURE THE AIRPLANE.

The commonality between the 757 and 767 is made apparent by the normal checklist, which is common to both aircraft types. *Author's collection*

newly issued Flight Standardization Board Report, officially designating the issuance and use of a pilot "common type rating" for the "B757/B767." That authorization permitted suitably qualified and trained pilots on either type to simultaneously receive both type ratings, allowing them to fly either type or both types, with both types automatically listed on their FAA pilot certificates. One day later, on July 20, the FAA FSB decision was reaffirmed by the chairman of the Flight Standardization Policy Board (FSPB). Then, on July 22 1983, the first B757/B767 common ratings were actually issued to the initial cadre of Boeing pilots and FAA Flight Standardization Board pilots. The additional rating was in turn added to any other pilot certificates of those pilots who up to that point in time had been issued only one type rating, in either the B757 or the B767. Now, regardless of which B757 or B767 rating a pilot had initially received, the other B757 or B767 rating was automatically added to their pilot certificate as appropriate. FAA Advisory Circular 61-86 was suitably modified to reflect the B757/B767 common type rating, and the rest is history.

As an epilogue, over the next decades, after we had issued that very first "B757/B767 common type rating," the process to assess a common rating and crew qualification ended up substantially driving increased flight deck commonality. That in turn spurred a profound and fundamental shift in flight deck design philosophy toward commonality. After this B757 and B767 CTR effort, commonality was increasingly sought as a goal in itself, to improve both safety and economy. That trend has beneficially lasted to this very day.

The CTR decision also implicitly spurred a massive improvement in aircraft systems toward commonality (FMSs, EFIS), use of common flight procedures (non-normal procedures), and formalization and simplification of training and differences training through commonality and credits. It ultimately led to further enhancements of the methodology itself for crew qualification assessment and testing. It served as the basis for modern-day authority criteria such as FAA Advisory Circular 120-53, for the determination of "Crew Qualification and Pilot Type Ratings" for any air transport aircraft, and, more recently, the internationally joint authority prescribed Joint Operations Evaluation Board. Those evolved criteria and improved assessment processes arguably have led to a significant improvement in flight safety. Commonality is an increasingly important foundation element, supporting the remarkably good flight safety record we now enjoy in modern commercial jet transport aircraft, and in airline flight operations globally.

INCREASED ENGINE EFFICIENCY

THE PRATT & WHITNEY PW2037

Pratt & Whitney's PW2037 offering was a bit late to the ball, but being an all-new design it had an optimized fan size specifically targeted for the 757's thrust requirements. The diameter of the fan was substantially larger than the RB.211, measuring out to 78.5 inches and increasing the bypass ratio to 5.8:1. This allowed a small measure of extra thrust (38,200 lbs.) with a specific fuel consumption improved by over 5% when compared to the -535C.

Since the PW2037 was an all-new engine and not a derivative of an older design, it took advantage of cutting-edge technology to the greatest extent possible and was equipped with an electronic management system called Full Authority Digital Engine Control (FADEC). The PW2037-powered 757-200 was the first Boeing jetliner to leave the factory with such a system, which is the industry standard today.

The Pratt & Whitney PW2037

Courtesy of the Boeing Company

Delta Air Lines took delivery of the first 757s equipped with the full FADEC Pratt & Whitney PW2037 engine. The engine can be easily differentiated from the Rolls-Royce RB.211-535C by the much-longer engine core protruding well aft of the fan cowl. *Courtesy of the Boeing Company*

Rolls-Royce RB.211 Traditional Engine Control

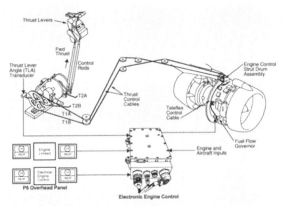

Pratt & Whitney PW2037 FADEC Engine Control

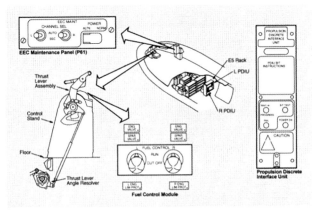

These diagrams illustrate the primary differences between the engine control systems of the more mechanically controlled Rolls-Royce RB.211 engine and the digitally controlled PW2037 engine. *Courtesy of the Boeing Company*

Prior to FADEC, jet engines used hydromechanical fuel controls, which supplied the engine's basic fuel metering. The fuel control for each engine was mechanically connected to the associated thrust lever in the cockpit by means of linkages, cables, and pulleys. In a typical "supervisory" system such as this, an electronic engine control (EEC) would schedule fuel additional to that provided by the hydromechanical system to optimize engine performance, particularly during rapid thrust changes. Although this system, as they say, "worked great and lasted a long time," it was complex and maintenance intensive, requiring mechanics to rig the cable system so that both thrust levers would be at exactly the same angle for the same amount of thrust. With FADEC, though, thrust could be precisely set without a need for constantly readjusting the thrust lever rigging to synchronize engine thrust settings. The 757's FADEC system was responsible for the following functions:

- basic engine operation, inclusive of starting, acceleration, deceleration
- speed governing
- stator vane control
- bleed valve control
- engine performance data
- fault detection
- management of the two control channels
- fault status indication for maintenance action

As always, safety was paramount, and each "worst-case scenario" had to be explored with the new system. It had to be ensured that electrical issues, including such rarities as static discharges and lightning strikes, would not adversely affect the FADEC system (and, thus, engine control). Jack Wimpress met with engineering representatives from Pratt & Whitney and Hamilton Standard, the producer of the PW2037 FADEC system. He saw that making the system

A close-up view of the PW2037 mounted to the 747 test aircraft. *Courtesy of the Boeing Company*

By June 1984, Ship 1 was converted for the certification testing of the 757 airframe powered by FADEC-controlled PW2037 engines. *Courtesy of the Boeing Company*

robust and bulletproof was going to be a difficult task, as he recounts: "So, I remember having time to go back and talk with them, and I got the failure modes and effects analysis from Project to take back there. And there was a roll of paper about 3 inches in diameter. I remember taking it to this meeting, and we were in this big conference room . . . full of people. They said, 'We don't see why this is such a tough problem.' I said, 'Well, here is the Failure Modes and Effects Analysis,' and I took that roll of paper and I rolled it out on the floor, and it went clear to the end of the conference room and bounced off the wall. These Pratt guys got up, started to read something, and say, 'Yeah, that's right,' and go down and read some more and they said, 'Yep, that's right.' By the time they had done that several times, they realized it really was a tough problem."

As part of the checks and balances required when designing and building new aircraft systems, Boeing didn't just rely on vendors but had its own experts in each field to hunt for potential problems. After exhaustively going through each possible failure mode, the team came up with a system that Wimpress described as being "a really good system."

Boeing used their 747 prototype aircraft to test the new engine and its FADEC system prior to flying it on the 757 airframe. The prototype 757 (N757A) was eventually modified too, with its original RB.211-535C engines being replaced by the new PW2037 power plants. Certification of the Pratt & Whitney engine on the 757 airframe was granted on October 25, 1984.

THE ROLLS-ROYCE RB.211-535E4

The 5% reduction in specific fuel consumption (SFC) offered by the PW2037, particularly in a time when oil companies were charging a healthy ransom for jet fuel, was enormous. This improvement spelled much-lower operating costs and the potential for longer-range capability as well. Rolls-Royce quickly realized that their RB.211-535C needed to be revamped into a more efficient version, or future sales of their engine on the 757 would likely be jeopardized.

By 1984, Rolls-Royce had introduced the "long cowl" version of their engine, called the RB.211-535E4. The SFC numbers of this upgraded version were essentially on par with the PW2037, though it was also capable of producing an improved 40,100 pounds of thrust at sea level. While the RB.211 had a reputation for being as tough as nails, it was still a derivative of the legacy engine (RB.211-524) used on all L-1011s and as an option on the 747. So, the RB.211-535E4, and later the -535E4B, having such an improvement of fuel consumption while still using a supervisory system (i.e., without a FADEC interface), was quite an accomplishment. Additionally, the -535B4 had the ability to produce nearly 2,000 additional pounds of thrust per engine, adding to the already exceptional takeoff-and-landing performance capability of the 757-200. FAA approval for the -535E4 on the 757 was granted on October 4, 1984, and it went on to be a heavily opted power plant for the 757.

The Rolls-Royce RB.211-535E4

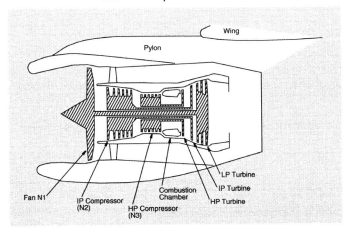

The Rolls-Royce RB.211-535E4 engine brought increased fuel efficiency, which allowed it to compete effectively with the PW2037. The E4 power plant went on to be a popular customer option. *Courtesy of the Boeing Company*

Eastern Airlines converted their 757 fleet to the more efficient RB.211-535E4 engine, which was easily discernible from the earlier 535C model by noting the longer fan cowl, masking the engine's core exhaust section. *Courtesy of the Boeing Company*

Once again, Boeing's 747 prototype was called into action for preliminary airborne testing of the Rolls-Royce RB.211-535E4 power plant. *Courtesy of the Boeing Company*

PASSENGER AND CARGO ACCOMMODATIONS

The power, performance, and lifting capability of the 757 allowed the use of 29-inch pitch seating, with a maximum passenger capacity of 239. The original door configuration, used on all of the first several 757s produced, allowed the highest passenger capacity available for the -200 series. This was limited by emergency egress limits rather than cabin size, even with high-density, 29-inch pitch seating.

Boeing realized that airlines wanted to optimize their cabins to suit their operation and their customers. To this end, a second 757 option, equipped with two overwing exits and three Type I doors per side, was developed in 1980 following the sale of the configuration to Delta Airlines. The initial 757 model, equipped with four Type I doors per side, was developed beginning with an official go-ahead in March 1979. The purpose of developing two configurations was to provide options to customers to optimize their seating arrangements. The "four-door" model had 178 seats in a standard, mixed-class arrangement, with the ability to seat up to 239 passengers in an exit-limited, high-density arrangement. The "overwing exit" model had 186 seats in a standard, mixed-class arrangement, with the ability to seat up to 224 passengers in a high-density arrangement based on FAA evacuation limits. Even though this configuration technically had more exits, a single Type I exit gave more passenger evacuation credit than two overwing hatches. However, because the Type I exits required a gap between the seating (where the overwing hatch configuration did not), this exit configuration allowed for an increase in galley storage volume from 0.95 cubic meters to 1.20 cubic meters, along with an additional lavatory. Following the commitment to Delta Airlines, the overwing exit model became the baseline used for competitive comparisons, starting with the thirty-seventh 757 built.

There was one further issue the 757 team had to resolve for using overwing hatches. While the trailing edge of the wing on the previous Boeing narrow bodies allowed for

WITH FOUR DOORS

239 PASSENGERS

WITH OVERWING EXITS

224 PASSENGERS

Courtesy of the Boeing Company

The aft galley accommodation aboard an Eastern Airlines 757. *Courtesy of the Boeing Company*

Boeing held a first-delivery ceremony for Delta's 757. Delta became a very prolific 757 customer despite initially being a potential launch customer for the proposed McDonnell Douglas DC-11, which, if built, would have been a direct competitor. The carrier would eventually operate a total of 205 different examples of the 757, inclusive of both the -200 and -300 series. *Courtesy of the Boeing Company*

passengers to egress and simply slide down the extended trailing edge flaps with a small jump to the ground, the 757 was much higher off the ground, necessitating an inflatable slide. Stowage for the slide was located in the wing-to-body fairing, just aft of the exits. Opening the overwing hatch automatically stowed the ground spoilers, inflated the slide, and illuminated the exterior emergency exit lights. The system was somewhat elaborate but was nonetheless effective.

The first 757 delivered with the overwing exit configuration was handed over to Delta Air Lines on November 5, 1984. This aircraft, N602DL (c/n 22809, l/n 39), was also the first PW2037-powered aircraft delivered as well.

Both door configurations proved to be popular but were rarely operated with seating for absolute maximum legal capacity. On the next page is an example of a more typical seating arrangement for both door configurations, with 36-inch seat pitch in first class and 32-inch pitch in economy.

N602DL (c/n 22809, l/n 39) was operated by Delta for nearly twenty-three years before being retired in 2017. *Courtesy of the Boeing Company*

This diagram shows the difference between the new "overwing exit" configuration (*top*) and the original "four-door" configuration for the 757. The overwing exit version increased usable cabin space because seats could be placed directly next to the overwing hatches. *Courtesy of the Boeing Company*

WITH OVERWING EXITS

12 FIRST CLASS   196 TOURIST

208 PASSENGERS

WITH FOUR DOORS

12 FIRST CLASS   190 TOURIST

202 PASSENGERS

A view of the interior of a Northwest Orient 757 from the first-class cabin, facing aft. *Courtesy of the Boeing Company*

Courtesy of the Boeing Company

Courtesy of the Boeing Company

Since the 757 was going to combine new levels of comfort with long-range capability, Boeing also offered the Inflight Video System to keep passengers entertained. The system consisted of seven monitors, evenly spaced throughout the cabin. The monitors gave a head clearance of 75 inches when retracted and 70 inches while in use, with their control unit being housed in the aft, left-side overhead bin.

BAGGAGE COMPARTMENTS

The 757-200 has two baggage compartments, one forward and one aft of the wing spar carry-through. The forward compartment has a standard capacity of 700 cubic feet and 10,300 pounds, with most of it located aft of the cargo door. A small staging area was also built in ahead of the door to facilitate more-convenient loading and unloading. The aft compartment (completely separated from the forward baggage stowage) was significantly larger, with 1,090 cubic feet of volume and a 16,300-pound weight limit.

To assist in providing the quickest turn capability possible, Boeing also offered the Telescoping Baggage System. This option allowed bags/cargo to be loaded close to the door, and then the sections would slide aft on rollers to expose the next section. This ease of loading did come with a slight price, though, since the telescoping assembly took up a small measure of volume, reducing the space in the forward compartment by 60 cubic feet, and in the aft by 40 cubic feet. This system, which originated on the 727, was a popular installation and by mid-1986 was in use by Air Europe, British Airways, Delta, Eastern, LTS, Republic, and Royal Brunei Airlines.

HINDSIGHT IS 20/20

One of the few traits that the 757 retained from the 727 airframe were the dimensions of the forward and aft fuselage and lower lobes. The smaller forward, lower lobe provided substantially less headroom than in the aft compartment, creating somewhat limited volume. However, there was a definite limit to how far forward the compartment could extend, since the aircraft's E/E bay (avionics compartment) was situated under the cockpit and around the nose landing gear well. Given the smaller 727 underbody, and the much-longer nose landing gear on the 757, electronics stowage was quite cramped, making electronics maintenance more difficult than on previous Boeing jets. Engineers looked for ways to solve the forward compartment volume issue, including using the deeper lower-lobe

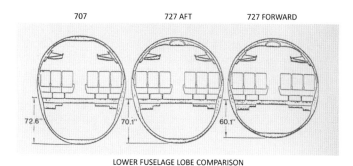

707   727 AFT   727 FORWARD

72.6"   70.1"   60.1"

LOWER FUSELAGE LOBE COMPARISON

Courtesy of the Boeing Company

This photo of China Southwest Airlines' B-2840 (c/n 27270, l/n 622) was taken in 1994 during high-altitude takeoff-and-landing trials at Bangda, China, which sits at an elevation of 14,206 feet above mean sea level. Normally, this is above the cabin altitude where the automatic passenger oxygen system would deploy the masks in the cabin! Note the supplemental oxygen being used by the test crew. *Courtesy of the Boeing Company*

section from the 707 to get the requisite volume. The initial aerodynamic drag estimates showed a 1% drag penalty, though, which was considered unacceptable. Jack Wimpress explains: "A lot of our aerodynamicists didn't believe that the drag was really that bad. The decision had to be made, so they made the decision to go with the smaller lower lobe. Later, we reran the wind tunnel tests and found that the testing was wrong the first time, and the drag was not that high. If that knowledge had been known, we probably would have put the deeper section on it. At the end of the program, Phil Condit, Jim Johnson, and I agreed that that was the worst mistake we made on that airplane. We created all kinds of problems. You couldn't stand up in the lower lobe with the baggage [handler] on his knees, and we crowded the E/E bay. We would have saved piles of dollars with a deeper lobe and a simpler E/E bay."

Today, many engineers agree with Wimpress on this issue. There was a further ramification from the shallow lobe too. To maximize the cargo capacity of the forward hold, the forward wing spar carry-through was moved slightly aft to allow the forward cargo compartment to extend farther in that direction. Since the center fuel tank was composed of the space between the forward and rear wing spar carry-throughs, this design change effectively shrunk volumetric fuel capacity. Later, after the introduction

of overwater ETOPS rules, the additional fuel capacity would have added to the range performance of the aircraft, easing transatlantic operations with the 757.

THE 757-200 HIGH-GROSS-WEIGHT OPTIONS

In an effort to make the 757 more versatile, (i.e., able to carry more payload, fuel, or both), Boeing offered higher weight options for the 757-200 from as far back as 1983. Although Boeing never officially designated these airplanes as "ER" (extended range), as they had with other types, many airlines adopted this designation, calling their aircraft the "Boeing 757-200ER."

Five different "flavors" would eventually be offered, since airlines desired increased takeoff and landing weights in order to utilize more of the aircraft's range capability while operating with higher payload weights. Compared to the aircraft's baseline 220,000-pound maximum takeoff weight (MTOW), the first 1983 option allowed an increase to 230,000 pounds, while another increase to 240,000 pounds was made available in 1984.

It is noteworthy that with all four takeoff weight versions of the 757-200, all shared the same maximum zero-fuel weight (MZFW) of 184,000 pounds. The MZFW, as the name implies, is the loaded weight of the aircraft without fuel. Similarly, the maximum landing gross weight (MLGW) also remained unchanged at 198,000 pounds. Given that this is the case, the MTOW increase without an associated MZFW or MLGW increase implies that the motivation was not to carry more weight in the cabin per se, but to carry it with more available fuel on board. With the adoption of ETOPS rules (as described in the next section), it made sense to carry more fuel for oceanic operations, as opposed to being weight limited and unable to carry a full payload.

By 2001, one further increase brought the MTOW to 255,000 pounds, but with this last option, the MZFW was also increased modestly to 184,000 pounds. Additionally, the MLGW was significantly increased to 210,000 pounds, offering some payload increase but even more room for fuel reserves. This option was offered with uprated versions of both the Pratt & Whitney PW2037 and Rolls-Royce RB.211-535E4 to provide additional lifting performance. The PW2040 engine was uprated from its predecessor, with a thrust increase from 36,600 to 40,100 pounds, while the RB.211-535E4B was likewise improved from 40,200 to 43,500 pounds of thrust.

These options substantially increased the range of the 757 airframe, from 2,430 (Basic) to 3,395 nautical miles for the highest-weight option with Pratt & Whitney engines. These improvements allowed for the 757 to become one of the most popular oceanic twin jets of the time.

EXTENDED-RANGE TWIN-ENGINE OPERATIONAL PERFORMANCE STANDARDS (ETOPS)

Since the dawn of powered flight, the power and reliability of aircraft engines have steadily improved. In the early years, engine failures were fairly common, but great strides were made in the years surrounding World War II to produce reliable power. Even still, in the postwar years it was not an uncommon sight to see a four-engine airliner landing with one engine shut down and its propeller feathered. Jet engines were developing quickly but were still relatively new technology and thus, for the most part, still unproven.

In 1953, the Civil Aeronautics Authority created a regulation that stated, "Unless approved by the administrator, a twin[-]engine airplane must stay within 60 minutes of a suitable alternate airport on one engine." This was an act of caution to protect the traveling public, but it did not apply to military operations. At the time, since large four-engine airplanes such as the Lockheed Constellation and Douglas DC-7 were the queens of transatlantic and transpacific travel, this regulation did not cause much of a stir in the airline industry.

As the jet age matured, jet engines had proven themselves quite reliable. Engine failures became an extremely low order of probability. In fact, they were much more reliable than the turbo-compound piston engines from just a few years before. Still, the regulation remained largely uncontested until the 1980s, when Boeing began selling the 757 and 767. The exceptional performance and range of these aircraft, which were originally intended for transcontinental use, made them ideal for transoceanic missions as well. The airplanes could certainly do the task, but the regulation would need to be changed to allow this new flexibility for the 757 and 767.

Dick Taylor, Boeing's vice president of product development and marketing management during this period, deeply believed that operating twin jets over the oceans was not only beneficial, but also ultimately safe. Taylor collected data on engine and aircraft systems reliability going back many years, leaving no stone unturned. Although he knew from his research that the old CAA rule was obsolete, the main challenge would be convincing the Federal Aviation Administration that a change needed to be made to reflect modern jetliner safety and reliability.

With the assistance of Boeing engineer Bob Bogash, Taylor went to the department heads within the company to determine what steps needed to be taken to ensure that the twin jet would be a superior overwater platform. Each department contributed to the writing of the document. Two studies, *Worldwide Operation of Twin-Jet Aircraft (Past, Present, and Future)* and *A Progress Report on Extended-Range Twin-Jet Operations*, were produced in 1983 and 1984, respectively. These reports took an in-depth look at "worst-case scenarios" for each aircraft system, and recommendations were also given to make each system even safer. Engine reliability and the reasons for the rare, in-flight engine shutdowns that had occurred were studied in depth. Additionally, when the sixty-minute rule was enacted, airport facilities were not nearly as refined when compared to modern aerodromes. Many of these airports used nonprecision approach procedures, which precluded landings with low clouds or poor visibility. With precision instrument landing systems (ILS) becoming more and more common around the world, this was another risk that Taylor and his team showed to have been largely mitigated. An additional source of leverage was that the ICAO, which governs aviation in numerous countries around the world, had already been running with ninety-minute alternate rules for years—further showing how outdated the sixty-minute rule was.

Although the FAA was reportedly resistant at first, through the combination of efforts and research by both Boeing and the FAA, one of the most significant advancements in commercial aviation history became reality. The new ETOPS rules required both the airline and the individual aircraft to be approved for long-range oceanic flights, starting with Trans World Airlines' new 767-200s.

They went on to fly the first FAA-sanctioned ETOPS flight, departing on February 1, 1985, from Boston, Massachusetts, with overwater routing to Paris's Charles de Gaulle Airport. The authorization allowed the airplane to be used to its full potential in operations from St. Louis, Missouri, to Frankfurt, West Germany, across the Atlantic Ocean, saving both time and fuel. Prior to this, twin jetliners would have to fly "the Blue Spruce Route," transiting Canada, Greenland, Iceland, and Scotland to stay within range of a sixty-minute alternate.

There were many naysayers who predicted problems with overwater twin-jet operations. While a common play on the ETOPS acronym was "Engines Turn or People Swim," history has shown that the research done by dedicated people at Boeing and the FAA has led to an unparalleled transoceanic safety record. In fact, overwater routes today are primarily flown by twin jets, with the last of the three- and four-engine airliners being retired in mass numbers. This is because twin jets not only have proven to be the safest platform but are also up to 6% more cost efficient than equivalent four-engine jets.

Since the 757's aircraft systems were already robust, few modifications had to be made on the ETOPS-certified aircraft. One such modification was in the electronics compartment, since without proper cooling it can become quite warm. This could lead to failure of avionics and aircraft systems equipment. As standard, the 757 was equipped with a cooling-fan system, but on the ETOPS aircraft, a second auxiliary fan was installed. Additional to this, a ram air turbine (RAT) was added in case of a failure of all electrical or all hydraulic power sources (or both). In this circumstance, the RAT deploys into the passing airflow to provide limited power to these aircraft systems. Finally, to aid in the intensive preventive-maintenance requirements set forth for ETOPS aircraft, a revised EICAS status-and-maintenance messaging system was included.

The introduction of ETOPS and, to some extent, US airline deregulation changed the way both the 757 and 767 were actually used in service. Boeing's Murray Booth sums up the ETOPS story and the effect that it had on

Boeing's newest twin jets: "Both airplanes were twins, and the interesting thing to me that is seldom discussed is that both airplanes were aimed at markets that didn't develop. They came into their own when they saw the longer-range North Atlantic service. They were designed pretty much with domestic markets in mind. The 7X7 was designed as a one-stop transcontinental airplane. Then we bucked up and said we need to make it nonstop transcontinental, Boston–San Francisco. We should also be able to get out of Denver and fly east. These were not the markets that made those airplanes successful. The markets developed later, [and these airplanes] created the market. It is interesting because during all of the arguments that determined these configurations, there was never any discussion to my recollection of where the airplanes would find their true home."

Bob Crandall, president of American Airlines, makes a deal with Boeing to buy fifty 757-200s in 1988. American became a major operator of the type, eventually operating a total of 177, inclusive of aircraft absorbed during the integration of America West Airlines, TWA, and US Airways. *Courtesy of the Boeing Company*

MORE SALES EFFORTS

Another major sales target for Boeing was American Airlines, which operated a large fleet of aging 727s. American had just acquired AirCal and inherited their 737 fleet as well, which the airline wished to replace with a newer-technology aircraft. Success was won on May 25, 1988, when American's leader, Bob Crandall, signed an order for fifty 757-200s, with options for fifty more. The order occurred the same week as another order from ILFC, an aircraft-leasing company, for one hundred more airplanes, with options for twenty more. The two orders combined were worth over $6.6 billion, showing that the 757 had come into its stride and was selling well.

The Boeing 757-200 had become a fast-selling airplane, offering airline customers many options, from seventeen different cabin configurations to multiple engine options. The adoption of ETOPS rules, along with exceptional fuel efficiency, made the 757 a highly desirable aircraft. Indeed, due its popularity and airframe capabilities, further versions of the 757 were just over the horizon.

This 757 (N615AM, c/n 24491, l/n 245) shows the aggressive takeoff performance for which the 757 was famous. N615AM was delivered new to American on September 12, 1989. The last 757 was retired from American's fleet in mid-2020 following the first few months of the coronavirus pandemic. *Courtesy of the Boeing Company*

CHAPTER 3
757 FREIGHTERS

THE 757PF (PACKAGE FREIGHTER)

The 757 was never intended to be sold as a pure cargo aircraft by the early program leaders. That being said, soon after the first 757-200s were delivered to their customers, some interest began to emerge for a freighter version of the aircraft. Boeing primarily targeted Federal Express, Flying Tigers, United Parcel Service (UPS), and DHL as freight carriers that might benefit from the greater efficiencies of a modern aircraft.

UPS showed the most interest in the aircraft, since their flight operation was expanding and they were considering the retirement of their older aircraft. They particularly liked the quiet operation of the 757's turbofan engines. Since freighters primarily flew at night, the public-relations aspect provided by operating the quiet 757 should not be underestimated.

The United States Postal Service was also intrigued, since much of their market share, particularly with express shipments,

had been taken by UPS and FedEx. It was believed that this interest was based on a plan to compete directly with these companies by utilizing modern equipment.

FedEx showed only mild interest in the 757 Package Freighter. They had a business plan that differed significantly from that of UPS. The management there saw more financial value in operating older aircraft that were nearly fully depreciated assets. In fact, this is what led to FedEx keeping their large fleet of 727-100s and -200s for several years. Many of these aircraft were converted with engine retrofits to bring noise and fuel consumption down.

Boeing estimated that a minimum sales figure to ensure profitability of this new 757 derivative was in the neighborhood of one hundred machines. The 757 Package Freighter was formally launched on December 30, 1985, with an order from UPS for twenty aircraft and fifteen additional options. The negotiated unit price was $31.5 million per aircraft, constituting the first-ever new aircraft order for the shipping giant.

An artist's rendering of the cargo-carrying 757 combi.
Courtesy of the Boeing Company

A cutaway drawing of the 757-200PF (Package Freighter). The small L1 crew access door is noteworthy. *Courtesy of the Boeing Company*

The 757 Package Freighter, given the internal Boeing designation 761-455, was much more than just a slightly modified passenger aircraft. The design's fuselage was completely devoid of the standard boarding and provisioning doors found on the passenger 757s. Instead, a large 134-by-86-inch cargo door was added forward of the port side wing. This allowed the easy on-and-off loading of fourteen 124-inch-wide by 88-inch-long cargo containers. The standard method used to restrain cargo in case of a failure of the pallet locks involved the use of a 9 g barrier net, located aft of the flight deck. UPS wanted to fit a fifteenth pallet into the aircraft, but the net took up too much space, so Boeing engineered a special cockpit bulkhead instead. This solution involved moving the pilot's entry door forward into the cockpit area, while also markedly reducing it in size to 22 by 55 inches. In addition to adding the necessary protection, it allowed space for up to five deadheading crew members, adding additional operational flexibility.

The main-deck cargo door is seen in the open position. The 757-200PF was completely devoid of passenger windows and standard entry doors. *Courtesy of the Boeing Company*

A view of the interior of the 757PF from an aft position, facing forward. *Courtesy of the Boeing Company*

This new aircraft featured a main-deck cargo volume of 6,610 cubic feet, while the under-floor cargo compartments were usable as well, adding 1,830 cubic feet of volume, slightly more than the standard 757. This was because UPS wanted the ability to carry an additional 900 gallons of fuel in an auxiliary fuel tank, situated in the forward portion of the aft baggage compartment. Still, a total of 87,650 pounds of payload could be carried in this configuration, enabled by an optional increase in maximum takeoff weight to 250,000 pounds.

One of the UPS's operational requirements involved being able to depart the shortest runway at their Louisville, Kentucky, sort hub, and to fly nonstop to the West Coast of the United States. UPS ultimately selected the Pratt & Whitney PW2040 engine, an uprated version of the PW2037, each providing 41,700 pounds of thrust to meet this requirement.

The rollout ceremony for the 757PF was held on July 15, 1987, with the first aircraft being delivered on September 17 of the same year. UPS would receive a total of five 757PFs in 1987, which were soon found to be extremely efficient. In comparison to the 757PFs, the 727-100Cs in use at the time were comparatively burning 112% more fuel per

Ethiopian Airlines operated a total of twelve 757s over the years, but ET-AJS (c/n 24845, l/n 300) was the sole 757-200PF acquired by the carrier. It is seen here prior to delivery to the airline on July 18, 1990. *Courtesy of the Boeing Company*

Many Boeing and UPS employees gathered to celebrate the delivery of the first 757-24APF aircraft (N401UP, c/n 23723, l/n 139) to the carrier in October 1987. *Courtesy of the Boeing Company*

available pound of payload. While FedEx was saving money on aircraft acquisitions, UPS was saving money on the basis of these efficiencies. Indeed, UPS was so impressed with their new airplane that they submitted an order for ten additional aircraft on March 16, 1989. All told, a total of eighty 757PFs were produced and delivered new from Boeing, most of which flew for UPS. While this fell somewhat short of the projected hundred-aircraft break-even point, it readily showed the capability of the 757 platform as a freighter.

THE 757M "COMBI"

On each of their previous jetliners, Boeing had achieved successes with the added operational flexibility brought with the use of convertible or "combi" aircraft. These airplanes are specially fitted to carry a combination of passengers and cargo. Some, such as the 727-100QC, allowed the movement of bulkheads to change the ratio of freight containers to passengers within minutes. Galleys, lavatories, and passenger seats were "palletized" and were simply rolled onto the aircraft and locked to the floor by using a special latching system.

Boeing wanted to offer this same level of flexibility for customers purchasing the 757. This airplane became known as the Boeing 757M (although some sources refer to it as a 757C) and had the same large cargo door installed forward of the left wing. The stock 757M could be flown in two configurations. The aircraft could be operated with a full passenger interior, or it could be quickly converted, with the partition moved aft, allowing for the carriage of two 88-by-108-inch cargo containers and 150 passengers, all seated aft of the L2 and R2 cabin doors.

The sole purpose-built 757-200M "combi" aircraft carried test registration N5573K during this predelivery departure from Renton Field's Runway 15. Due to magnetic polar shift, this runway was redesignated Runway 16 in August 2009. *Courtesy of the Boeing Company*

This photo is taken from the 757-200M forward cabin, facing aft. Note the extended flight and ground spoilers. *Courtesy of the Boeing Company*

The newly built forward fuselage section, inclusive of the large main-deck cargo door, is lowered into position for installation. *Courtesy of the Boeing Company*

The airliner market had changed with the times, though, and only one factory-built 757M was sold. This airplane (c/n 22863, l/n 182) was given test registration N5573K and was delivered new to Royal Nepal Airlines, registered as 9N-ACB on September 15, 1988.

BOEING AIRPLANE SERVICES AND THE 757SF (SPECIAL FREIGHTER)

To attract the carriers such as DHL and FedEx, Boeing Airplane Services saw the potential of converting previously owned 757-200s into pure freighters. The converted aircraft, marketed as the 757SF, would meet the desires of those carriers who wished to operate used aircraft that were largely depreciated assets, while still taking advantage of the 757's efficiency. The 757SF program was launched with an order from DHL on October 15, 1999, for the conversion of forty-four aircraft.

There was, however, one minor disadvantage associated with the 757SF conversion when compared to the 757PF. Since all of the 757SF aircraft were produced in a passenger aircraft configuration, the forward boarding and galley doors (L1 and R1, respectively) needed to be retained, as opposed to having the smaller door located in the cockpit of the 757PF. This required the cargo bulkhead to be located a few feet farther aft, reducing the maximum pallet capacity from fifteen to fourteen, though it was still capable of carrying 60,000 pounds of cargo.

Boeing completed the conversions at its facility in Wichita, Kansas, and the first flight of the 757SF was conducted from this facility on February 15, 2001. As time went on, the 757 freighter conversions were also handled by Israel Aerospace Industries (IAI), Precision Aircraft Solutions, and ST Aerospace Services.

Precision Aircraft Solutions, headquartered in Beaverton, Oregon, markets their 757 pure-freighter conversion as the 757PCF, while they also offer a "combi" conversion called the 757PCC, which allows the flexibility to carry combinations of passengers and freight. Carriers such as Air China, Air Transport International, DHL, and Icelandair have operated aircraft with these conversions, which are conducted in Portland, Oregon.

ST Aerospace of Singapore offers a similar modification, under a supplemental type certificate authorization to convert passenger 757s to pure freighters. In January 2007, FedEx ordered eighty-seven 757 conversions, with deliveries conducted over a seven-year period. Subsequently, DHL has also ordered conversions from ST Aerospace. Their offerings come as three different conversion options:

- pure freighter with standard passenger forward exits and a 14.5-container capacity
- pure freighter with 757PF-type crew entry door and capacity for fifteen containers
- Combi configuration with capacity for eight containers (forward) and eighty passengers (aft cabin)

Three 757-200s were converted from a pure passenger interior into a Combi configuration. These aircraft, N752CX (c/n 24451, l/n 227), N753CX (c/n 26152, l/n 478), and N754CX (c/n 26154, l/n 486), were previously operated by National Airlines (III) prior to the carrier ceasing operations. ATI contracted PEMCO to complete the Combi conversions on these machines, which had some additional flexibility when compared to the sole 757M built by Boeing. There were six different loading configurations possible, which allowed up to 65,401 pounds of cargo (dependent upon pallet dimensions) to be carried, with a passenger compartment located behind the wing, aft of the Type II emergency exits.

These conversions proved to be quite popular with the world's freight carriers. As the 727 and DC-8 freighter fleets aged, many carriers replaced them with cargo-carrying 757s. As of July 2020, a total of 315 757 freighters were in operation, four of which are Combi aircraft, including the sole 757M built for Royal Nepal Airlines, as noted earlier.

CHAPTER 4
THE 757 IN MILITARY AND GOVERNMENT SERVICE

An unidentified C-32A lifts off from Renton Field. The US Air Force states that one advantage of the C-32A is its high stance on the ramp, making visibility for security purposes much easier than with most other aircraft types. *Courtesy of the Boeing Company*

THE C-32A

The United States government saw the need for an aircraft type to replace the aging VC-137s, which were based on the legacy Boeing 707. These were used to transport upper-level government officials, including the president and vice president. Boeing's answer was to use the 757-200 airframe as the basis for the new transport. Four of these airplanes, designated as C-32As, were ordered, with the first delivery to the USAF 89th Airlift Wing occurring on June 1, 1998. This aircraft was registered 98-0001 (tail 80001, c/n 29025, l/n 783) and was soon followed by 98-0002 (tail 80002, c/n 29026, l/n 787), 99-0003 (tail 90003, c/n 29027, l/n 824), and 99-0004 (tail 90004, c/n 29028, l/n 829), to complete the order.

The C-32A provides accommodation for forty-five passengers and sixteen crew members and has proven itself capable of flights up to 6,160 nautical miles. This additional range is allowed by the use of four under-floor auxiliary fuel tanks, installed for international missions. Intended

Passenger and Crew Accommodations

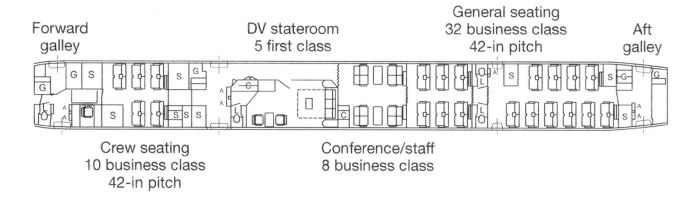

Forward galley

DV stateroom
5 first class

General seating
32 business class
42-in pitch

Aft galley

Crew seating
10 business class
42-in pitch

Conference/staff
8 business class

Courtesy of the Boeing Company

to literally be a flying White House, GTE AIRFONES are provided at each seating station.

The US government naturally selected the indigenous Pratt & Whitney PW2040, with a maximum approved takeoff thrust of 41,700 pounds. Unlike its jetliner counterparts, though, the C-32's time at maximum power was doubled to ten minutes instead of the standard five. Since the C-32A was to be operated in some "not-so-friendly" regions of the world, this additional maximum thrust allowance permitted the aircraft to spend minimal time at low altitudes, where there was greater risk of exposure to enemy fire. The C-32A was approved for a maximum takeoff weight of 255,000 pounds to account for the extra weight from the auxiliary tanks, but could still operate from a 7,000-foot runway with a full load. Even with all of these performance improvements, the C-32A remained stage III noise compliant, which is definitely important for a diplomatically oriented aircraft.

C-32A tail 80001 was delivered to the US Air Force in June 1998. Today, this airplane has been retrofitted with blended winglets, increasing range and fuel efficiency. This aircraft can carry 92,000 pounds of fuel by using auxiliary tanks. *Courtesy of the Boeing Company*

THE P-3C ORION REPLACEMENT AIRCRAFT

The United States Navy was interested in replacing their fleet of Lockheed P-3C maritime antisubmarine reconnaissance aircraft. Lockheed, naturally, wanted to be the heir apparent and submitted a design that was, for all intents and purposes, a scaled-up P-3C, an airframe based on the L-188 Electra design dating back to the 1950s. British Aerospace likewise submitted a proposal for a somewhat modernized version of the Nimrod, based on an even-earlier design, the de Havilland Comet. This all makes perfect sense given that such aircraft would be ordered in very small numbers and would not justify the construction of an entirely new airframe type.

Boeing initially came to the party for the proposed P-7, with a 757-200 airframe, adorned with all of the electronic-warfare equipment required. The design called for three

Courtesy of the Boeing Company

Courtesy of the Boeing Company

The Boeing P-8, a 737 Next Generation–based aircraft, is currently replacing the venerable Lockheed P-3C. *Courtesy of the Boeing Company*

underbody ordinance bays, one forward of the wing and two side by side, aft of the wing. Additional to this, four hardpoints were to be installed on the wings to increase its military capability. While Boeing did win in the end, it was years later and with an entirely different airframe. The Navy's newest patrol aircraft, the P-8 Poseidon, is based on the 737-800 series. It possessed load-carrying improvements inherited from the 737-900 and special wingtips, optimized for the low-level loitering that anti-submarine operations demand.

N757A: THE 757 PROTOTYPE AND FLYING TEST BED

The Boeing 757-200 prototype airplane, N757A (c/n 22212, l/n 1), has remained as a Boeing-owned flying test bed throughout the years. One of the major tasks given to this aircraft was to test avionics and weapon systems for the Lockheed F-22 "Raptor" Advanced Tactical Fighter program. Boeing held the bulk of the responsibility for the avionics package for the new fighter jet. As such, work began in April 1990, using Boeing Field as a base of operations. The use of the 757 test bed aircraft allowed problems to be identified and solutions to be found rapidly, long before the F-22's first flight in 1997.

Going one step further for the next phase of the project, in August 1999, N757A was heavily modified by having an F-22 nose literally grafted onto its airframe. While the stock 757 has a bit of a "bird of prey" stance to it already, this modification removed any remaining doubts. The test bed was initially flown with only the F-22 nose and various sensors, but soon thereafter a "wing" assembly was added to the top of the forward fuselage, similar in appearance to a canard. The intent of this modification was not aerodynamic per se, but instead to provide a place for testing the F-22's wing-mounted sensors. As part of the testing, a functional F-22 cockpit was also added inside the 757's cabin to allow for the most realistic testing possible. As of 2020, this aircraft was still in use as an advanced avionics test bed, improving military aviation technology.

Ship 1 seen in flight as the avionics test bed for the F-22 program. *Courtesy of the Boeing Company*

By this point, Ship 1 had "grown" an F-22-esque nose to further test the new fighter's avionics. *Courtesy of the Boeing Company*

A close-up view of Ship 1 with the F-22 nose fairing. *Courtesy of the Boeing Company*

Ship 1 was finally able to test the full avionics suite for the F-22, including the wing-mounted sensors that were added with the use of a fairing above the flight deck. Note that this aircraft is still equipped with the PW2037-series engine type that it tested in 1984. *Courtesy of the Boeing Company*

NASA'S 757

In 1994, the National Air and Space Administration (NASA) acquired a 757 for use as the Airborne Research Integrated Experiments System (AIRES). The airframe chosen was c/n 22191, l/n 002, which was the first production 757 built and was operated by Eastern Airlines as N501EA. According to NASA, this airplane was used as an airborne laboratory to test systems to enhance the safety and efficiency of the world's airspace systems. As part of this, advancements for the Air Traffic Services (ATS) system were evaluated in relation to advanced airborne avionics. In January 2009, this airplane was placed in storage until being taken up by Starflite International Corporation in April of that same year, reregistered as N144DC.

NASA's 757 had a cabin packed with test equipment, used to further aviation technology and safety. *Courtesy of the Boeing Company*

N557NA clearly shows its former life as an Eastern Airlines jet. *Courtesy of the Boeing Company*

The Boeing 757 embodied a rare combination of excellent performance and fuel efficiency. These traits made this airplane a popular jetliner, while also making it an ideal platform for government use as well as for research-and-development purposes. Capable of conducting a swift climb from a short runway, then traveling great distances unrefueled, the 757 was largely unmatched by other jetliners and lent itself well to specialized missions.

CHAPTER 5
THE 757-300 SERIES

The 757-200 was a remarkably capable jetliner with an exceptionally strong airframe and an abundance of performance. When compared to the legacy 727, it demonstrated an improvement of 46% on direct operating costs per seat. Even though the 757 was quite efficient on shorter trips of just 500 nautical miles, Boeing still saw the opportunity to lower operating costs even more.

Fuselage stretches are the simplest and most effective way of decreasing seat-mile costs. In fact, Boeing had successfully used this technique on each of its previous jetliner series, including the 747, which had a stretched upper deck on its -300- and -400-series aircraft. Stretching the 757 would prove to be a reasonably simple modification because of three primary factors. First, its wing-mounted engines made the 757 well balanced by the nature of its design, allowing simple fuselage stretches forward and aft of the wing without causing weight and balance problems. Second, the 757's low-set horizontal stabilizers, when compared to a T-tail configuration, do not manifest any deep stall issues that can come with fuselage stretches, as we saw in chapter 2. Last, the 757-200 had a rather long landing gear, providing

THE 757-300 SERIES   115

Courtesy of the Boeing Company

Boeing 757-300
Changes relative to the Boeing 757-200

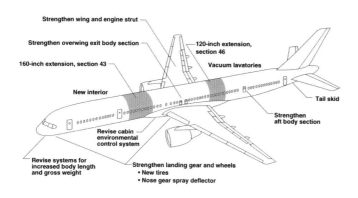

Courtesy of the Boeing Company

structural reinforcements to the wing and center fuselage section in order to bear the extra loads. The landing gears were strengthened, and new wheels, twenty-six-ply tires, and upgraded brakes were added as well.

To help prevent damage to the aft fuselage, primarily during takeoff, a retractable tail skid was incorporated into the design. A body contact indicator, similar to the one used on the 777, was also installed to allow the aircraft to continue to its destination in case of a light-tail-skid-to-runway contact during rotation on takeoff.

Recall that the 757-200 was offered with two different door configurations, one with the use of a Type I exit installed behind the wing on each side of the fuselage, and the other with overwing exits and inflatable slides for emergency evacuations. The 757-300, with a passenger capacity set for 280 passengers, would require more exits to meet FAA regulations for egress. On the 757-300, Boeing

plenty of tail clearance with the runway during takeoff and landing. Boeing's Jack Wimpress remembers a conversation that he had with revered aircraft designer Ed Wells during the design of the 757-200: "He sat down in my office and he said, 'You know, we fought like crazy on the 707 to get the shortest possible landing gear that we could have, because landing gear length is all about weight.' And when Douglas stretched the DC-8 into the 60 series, Boeing couldn't follow them because we had built ourselves into a corner that we couldn't get out of. And he said, 'Don't make your landing gear too short.' We followed that advice. It has a relatively long landing gear and allowed the 757-300 to be built."

The expanded capacity for the 757-300 was accomplished by adding a 160-inch fuselage plug ahead of the wing, and a 120-inch extension aft. This increased the length from 155 feet, 3 inches, to 178 feet, 7 inches, raising the cabin volume and passenger capacity by 20% while also increasing the under-floor baggage/cargo space by 50%.

The same wing planform was used, but with the maximum takeoff weight increased to 272,500 pounds, necessitating

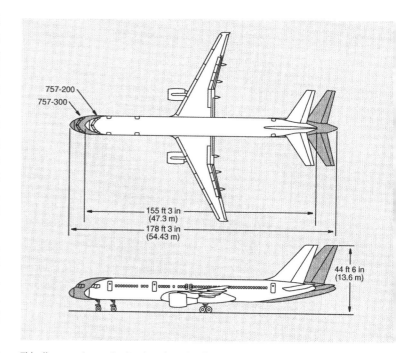

This diagram shows the fuselage length difference between the 757-200 and 757-300. *Courtesy of the Boeing Company*

Due to the fuselage extension of the 757-300, a retractable tail skid (*green arrow*) was integrated into the design to help prevent damage from an aggressive rotation during takeoff. *Courtesy of the Boeing Company*

This Condor 757-300 was equipped for overwater operations with these overhead-stowed rafts. *Courtesy of the Boeing Company*

used a combination of the two configurations, with both the overwing exits and the two additional Type I exits to support the additional capacity.

The interior for the 757-300 was based on that of the then-new 737 Next Generation series. This featured a modernized cabin ceiling, larger overhead bins, and vacuum lavatories. The vacuum-powered toilets used potable water for flushing instead of the traditional lavatory fluid. On the old system, the ramp agent would have to dump the waste tank and then refill it with fluid. Since the new system used only potable water, the last step was unnecessary.

During the Farnborough Airshow on September 2, 1996, the German charter operator Condor Flugdienst effectively launched the program by submitting an order for twelve Rolls-Royce-powered 757-300s. Shortly thereafter, the 757-300 design reached a firm configuration on November 15, 1996, with an anticipated first delivery to Condor in January 1999. This left only twenty-seven months to produce the aircraft, at the time making it the fastest schedule of any Boeing aircraft derivative, with the exception of the 737-400 series.

The official rollout ceremony for the 757-300 occurred on May 31, 1998. Dr. Dietmar Kirchner, the managing

The 757-300 used a combination of the two 757-200 exit configurations to allow a maximum capacity of 280 passengers. *Courtesy of the Boeing Company*

757-300

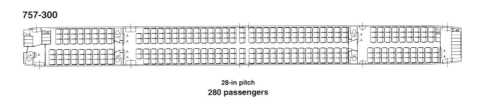

28-in pitch
280 passengers

This photo of the Renton assembly hall shows the obvious difference in size
between the 757-200 in the background and the 757-300 in the foreground.
Courtesy of the Boeing Company

Another view of the final assembly of a 757-300. *Courtesy of the Boeing Company*

The festive rollout ceremony of the 757-300 prototype. *Courtesy of the Boeing Company*

Joe Sutter had identified that the 757 nose shape resembled the DC-8's during the aircraft's development. The stretched 757 can be said to bear some resemblance to the stretched DC-8-60 series from many angles. *Courtesy of the Boeing Company*

director of Condor, expressed great confidence in the new airplane, telling the crowd that it had the lowest seat-mile costs of any narrow-body aircraft. With that, on the spot, he submitted an order for one additional airplane, bringing the total for the airline up to thirteen.

757-300 FIRST FLIGHT

On August 2, 1998, the 757-300 first took to the skies for a two-hour and thirty-five-minute flight under the command of Captains Leon Roberts and Jerry Whites from Renton, Washington, after a month of delays. Since the runway at Renton is quite short for a large jet, at only 5,382 feet in length, the airplane was operated at only 186,400 pounds, which is fairly light for a jetliner of its size. The flight went quite well, although the static cone installed for instrument calibration purposes became detached. Aerodynamic stalls and preliminary flutter tests were conducted, and the aircraft performed nicely in both areas. This ship was given test registration N757X (D-ABOA, c/n 29016, l/n 804) and was the first of three airplanes to participate in the certification testing. It would soon be accompanied by N6076B (D-ABOB, c/n 29017, l/n 810) and N1787B (D-ABOC, c/n 29015, l/n 818). Together, these airplanes conducted 1,286 hours of ground testing and 912 hours of flight evaluation.

Joint FAA/JAA certification was granted in January 1999, and for the second time in history (the 777-200 being the first), "out of the box" ETOPS authorization was granted.

Courtesy of the Boeing Company

A system of water barrels, lines, and pumps are used to change the center of gravity (CG) of the aircraft while in flight by pumping water forward and aft as needed. This often saves the need to land and redistribute weight in the cabin. *Courtesy of the Boeing Company*

D-ABOG (c/n 29014, l/n 849) is seen during predelivery preparations. This aircraft was delivered to the German carrier on March 19, 1999. *Courtesy of the Boeing Company*

It is also interesting that the 757-300 was the first aircraft certified using a project-specific certification plan. This plan signifies an agreement between the FAA and Boeing that involved setting twenty-four specific milestones to keep the program on schedule.

757-300 HIGH-GROSS-WEIGHT OPTION

As with the 757-200, there was a desire to achieve as much full-cabin range for the 757-300 as possible. The available thrust increases from the uprated PW2043 and RB.211-535E4B power plants allowed for a substantial improvement to be offered by 2001. The maximum takeoff weight with this heaviest option was 273,000 pounds, as opposed to the 240,000 pounds for the basic model. The operational range with reserves for the Pratt & Whitney–powered aircraft was extended from 2,120 to 3,395 nautical miles, while the maximum landing and zero-fuel weights remained the same, at 224,000 and 210,000 pounds, respectively.

When the 757-300 launched, its fuel efficiency was second to none in the narrow-body world. By the time it was certified in 1999, though, Boeing's backlog of orders was beginning to wane, and the financial chaos in the airline industry after 9/11 was leading to airlines downsizing and canceled orders. All of this, along with the subsequent cancellation of the Boeing 757 program, meant that only fifty-five 757-300s were ever delivered.

CHAPTER 6
757s IN SERVICE

The production of 757s and 727s overlapped from December 1979, when first metal was cut for the 757 prototype, until August 1984, when the last 727 was delivered to Federal Express. Ship 2 (N501EA, c/n 22191, l/n 2) shares the ramp with a brand-new 727-225 (N820EA, c/n 22557, l/n 1795). Both aircraft made their maiden flights in March 1982. *Courtesy of the Boeing Company*

The year 1984 was a period of transitions at Boeing. The early 757s were being delivered with the last of the 727-200s. Concurrent with this was the production of the first of the 737-300 series alongside the last of the 737-200 Advanced machines. *Courtesy of the Boeing Company*

Air Europe was an early customer for the 757-200. This airplane (G-BKRM, c/n 22176, l/n 14) was first delivered to the carrier on March 30, 1983. It was operated by the airline until 1989 but was leased on occasion to British Airways during times of low demand. The airplane changed hands multiple times and is currently operated by Southwest Sportsjet in Anchorage, Alaska. *Courtesy of the Boeing Company*

Northwest Orient took delivery of this 757-251 (N508US, c/n 23197, l/n 69) on August 23, 1985, which was an early Pratt & Whitney–powered example. Ship 508 was scrapped in 2012. *Courtesy of the Boeing Company*

Republic Airlines was formed as the first airline "merger" after the passage of
the US Airline Deregulation Act, when North Central Airlines and Southern
Airways joined forces. Later, the carrier merged with Hughes Airwest prior to
purchasing the 757 to replace their fleet of aging 727-200s. Republic merged with
Northwest Airlines in 1986, during the period's merger mania. N602RC (c/n 23322,
l/n 79) endured the merger with Northwest but soon left the fleet to serve with
America West Airlines as N902AW, which in turn was transferred to US Airways
and finally American Airlines due to airline acquisitions. *Courtesy of the Boeing
Company*

LTU Sud operated this 757-2G5 (D-AMUW, c/n 23929, l/n 153) from late 1987
until 2004. Today, the aircraft is operated by FedEx as N943FD and has been
converted to a pure freighter. *Courtesy of the Boeing Company*

The Spanish carrier Iberia operated a total of forty-three 757-200s throughout the years. This airplane (EC-HDS, c/n 26252, l/n 900) was delivered new to the carrier in 1999 and served with the airline until 2006. Today, it is operated by Privilege Style Airlines, a Spanish charter carrier. *Courtesy of the Boeing Company*

This 757-2Zo (B-2845, c/n 27512, l/n 674) was purchased by China Southwest Airlines but was transferred to China National Aviation Corporation prior to delivery. In 2012, this airplane was converted to a freighter and is currently operated by SF Airlines under the same registration. *Courtesy of the Boeing Company*

Boeing jets had gained the respect of the Moroccan monarchy over the years. King Hassan II had even survived an armed attack from renegade Northrop F-5 fighters in a Boeing 727 and landed safely, prompting him to give the machine the Wissam al-Arch (Order of the Throne), an award normally reserved for the most-deserving humans. Royal Air Maroc acquired this 757-2B6 (c/n 23686, l/n 103) on July 15, 1986, which served with the carrier until being stored in 2010. *Courtesy of the Boeing Company*

ET-AJX (c/n 25014, l/n 348) was acquired by Ethiopian Airlines on February 25, 1991, and was converted into a freighter in 2006. *Courtesy of the Boeing Company*

United Airlines was a major 757 operator, eventually operating a total of 160 examples. Even in the 2020–21 pandemic era, the carrier still operates thirteen 757-200s (a mix of United and Continental airplanes) and sixteen 757-324s, which came from the Continental merger. N541UA (c/n 25253, l/n 394) left United in 2014 and currently serves as a 757-222SF with FedEx. *Courtesy of the Boeing Company*

THE 757 AND WAKE TURBULENCE

The Boeing 757 had established itself by the early 1990s with an excellent in-service record, handling that was loved by pilots, and economics that were enjoyed by airline leadership. Although it was considered an extremely safe aircraft itself, the dynamics of its design could occasionally present a problem for other aircraft.

Aircraft, like their watercraft cousins, leave wake turbulence in their path. As a generality, like their seagoing counterparts, the larger an aircraft is, the stronger its wake turbulence will be. Following this logic, there are regulatory requirements for in-trail distancing between arriving and departing aircraft, on the basis of the size classifications involved. An aircraft with a maximum takeoff weight of over 300,000 pounds was considered a "heavy" aircraft and is accordingly referred to as such during radio calls, such

as "Speedbird 1 *heavy*," to alert other aircraft of the potential wake hazard.

While some of the wake close to the aircraft is caused by jet engine efflux, the more significant issue is the turbulence generated by the airframe. Wings allow aircraft to fly because, by design, there is higher air pressure beneath the wing. At the wingtip, the high-pressure air from underneath spills over the wingtip to attempt to equalize the pressure. By the time this occurs, though, the movement of the wingtip means it's already gone, resulting in a small tornado being formed by each wingtip. As a general rule, notwithstanding atmospheric conditions, the heavier the aircraft, the longer the wake lasts. The 757-200 turned out to produce much-stronger wake turbulence than other aircraft in its size class (255,000 pounds).

In the time period of 1992 through 1993, three aircraft mysteriously lost control while following 757s on approach—a

Cessna 182, a Cessna Citation, and an IAI Westwind executive jet. Research into these accidents showed that the 757 packed a bigger punch than was previously thought. Reported issues became more common because of greater traffic saturation in terminal areas, and, with new 757s entering service every month, the FAA realized that solving the issue required special rule making. The latest version of the law, order JO 7110.126A, essentially put the 757 in the same separation class with much-larger aircraft such as 747s and DC-10s. Air traffic controllers abiding by the rule change would now allow two minutes of separation between a 757 and smaller aircraft operating in-trail. While wake turbulence still exists, it is largely mitigated today through increased distances and a greater understanding of its effects.

N509US (c/n 23198, l/n 70) demonstrates the impressive takeoff performance of the 757-200. *Courtesy of the Boeing Company*

Singapore Airlines took delivery of this 757-212 (9V-SGK, c/n 23125, l/n 44) on November 11, 1984. In 1990, this ship was transferred to American Trans Air as N751AT, and then to Delta Air Lines in 1996. The aircraft was retired from service in 2016. *Courtesy of the Boeing Company*

RIGHT: America West Airlines began service on August 1, 1983, with a small fleet of Boeing 737 Original-series aircraft. N907AW (c/n 22691, l/n 155) was delivered on December 10, 1987, and served with the Phoenix-based carrier until 2006. In 2009, this airplane was converted into a pure freighter and is now flown by FedEx as N941FD. *Courtesy of the Boeing Company*

American Trans Air (ATA) operated many exotic charters but also operated regular scheduled service. This festive paint scheme was applied to N520AT (c/n 27976, l/n 814), which was operated by the carrier until its bankruptcy and the subsequent purchase of remaining assets by Southwest Airlines in 2008. The aircraft went on to fly for Ethiopian Airlines before being acquired by DHL in 2016. *Courtesy of the Boeing Company*

Uzbekistan Airlines has operated a total of eleven 757-200s over time. This airplane, VP-BUB *Urgench* (c/n 30060, l/n 875), first took flight on June 29, 1999, and was delivered to the carrier the following September. With a registration change to UK75701, the airplane was stored in 2019. *Courtesy of the Boeing Company*

Azerbaijan Airlines operated this 757-22L (VP-BBS, c/n 30834, l/n 947) from December 2000 until May 2020. *Courtesy of the Boeing Company*

Delta took delivery of N6701 (c/n 30187, l/n 892) in 1999 and repainted it to reflect Delta's "Official Olympic Carrier" status for the 2002 Salt Lake City games. This airplane was later repainted for Delta's short-lived "Song" operation, before becoming "mainline" again in 2006. This airplane was stored in the wake of the 2020–21 pandemic. *Courtesy of the Boeing Company*

National Airlines (III) was an airline based in Las Vegas, Nevada, that operated a fleet of nineteen 757-200s from 1999 to 2002. N558NA (c/n 32446, c/n 950) was never taken up by the carrier and was instead delivered to Air 2000 in February 2001. Today, this airplane is operated by TUI Airways as G-OOBA. *Courtesy of the Boeing Company*

Even during the height of the Cold War, the Chinese saw the value of a Boeing airplane. This aircraft (B-2801, c/n 24014, l/n 144) was delivered to China Southern Airlines on September 22, 1987, and served with the carrier until 2006. *Courtesy of the Boeing Company*

Arguably the most famous 757 built, OY-SHA (c/n 25155, l/n 371) was purchased new by Sterling Airways, a Danish charter carrier, from Boeing in 1991. Since 2011, American businessman (and later president of the United States) Donald J. Trump has used this airplane (reregistered as N757AF) as a personal and business transport. *Courtesy of the Boeing Company and Tomas Del Coro via Wikimedia Commons (https://commons.wikimedia.org/wiki/File:N757AF_at_LAS.jpg-Unmodified)*

American Trans Air operated a total of thirty-six Boeing 757s, including ten 757-33Ns. This aircraft (N555TZ, c/n 32589, l/n 1003) was delivered to the airline February 28, 2002. Just over one year later, ATA declared bankruptcy and ceased operations. Reregistered as N77865, this airplane went to fly for Continental Airlines and is currently operated by United Airlines. *Courtesy of the Boeing Company*

D-ABOM (c/n 29022, l/n 926) is seen on final approach with Condor's modernized paint scheme advertising their partnership with the Thomas Cook travel group. *Courtesy of Wo st 01 via Wikimedia Commons (https://commons.wikimedia.org/wiki/File:Condor_B757-30_D-ABOM_EDDF.jpg, Unmodified)*

Northwest Airlines was an early operator of the Pratt & Whitney–powered 757, taking their first aircraft directly from Boeing in February 1985. In addition to its large fleet of 757-200-series aircraft, the carrier also operated sixteen 757-351s. This airplane (N583NW, c/n 32983, l/n 1019) was one of the last 757s built. Today, this airplane is still active with Delta Air Lines. *Courtesy of Josveo5A via Wikimedia Commons (https://commons.wikimedia.org/wiki/File:THE_Boeing_757-300_(385585503).jpg, Unmodified)*

Arkia Israeli Airlines was formed in 1949, shortly after the establishment of the nation of Israel. This 757-3E7 was delivered new to the carrier on January 31, 2000. After nineteen years of dependable service with Arkia, today it is operated by Azur Air Ukraine as UR-AZP. *Courtesy of Saarb737 via Wikimedia Commons (https://commons.wikimedia.org/wiki/File:Arkia_B757-300WL_4X-BAU.jpg, Unmodified)*

Seen departing Los Angeles International Airport with its landing gear just beginning the retraction sequence, N57857 (c/n 32816, l/n 1040) was delivered new to Continental Airlines in 2004, prior to its merger with United Airlines in 2010. Courtesy of Magnus Manske via Wikimedia Commons (https://commons.wikimedia.org/wiki/File:United_Airlines_Boeing_757-300_N57857_(6405375609)_(2).jpg, Unmodified)

Delta acquired N584NW (c/n 32984, l/n 1020) during the carrier's merger with Northwest Airlines in 2008. Courtesy of Tyler ser Noche via Wikimedia Commons (https://commons.wikimedia.org/wiki/File:Delta_N584NW_Boeing_757-300_ATL_Sep2017_(43590005660).jpg, Unmodified)

THE END OF THE 757 PROGRAM?

April 28, 2005, marked the end of 757 production as the final aircraft (B-2876, c/n 33967, l/n 1050) was delivered to Shanghai Airlines. In total, 1,050 Boeing 757s of all variants were produced in a production run that spanned twenty-five years. The program was halted due to declining sales even as sales of the once-struggling 737 soared. Another factor that may have influenced this decision was that both airplanes were being built in the Renton assembly hall, and space for the accelerating 737 production was at a premium.

The Boeing 737 is a fine aircraft—safe, durable, and efficient. It began life as a short-range aircraft, designed to bring jet service to communities that had never experienced such luxuries. The original series 737-200 was even capable of operating from unimproved airfields, bringing service to remote locations in Alaska, Canada, Africa, and South America. Over the years, the 737 design had grown into an aircraft that had increased fuel capacity and range, with the largest version, the 737-900ER (then

This 757-26D (c/n 33967, l/n 1050) was the 1,050th Boeing 757 built—the last of the breed. Delivered on April 26, 2005, this airplane signaled the end of 757 production and has been operated by Delta Air Lines as N823DX since 2016. Courtesy of the Boeing Company via Duane Jackson

in development), having a cabin capacity nearly as large as the 757-200. Although the 737 lacked the rocket-like performance of the 757, it was capable of reliably operating from the West Coast of the United States to the Hawaiian Islands under ETOPS rules. Airbus was also in the arena with its A321, which was close in size and shared a range capability similar to the 737-900ER. Both of these aircraft could perform many of the missions that were being served by the 757, but with lower direct operating costs due to their updated wings and engines.

It is also widely believed that the ideal size of the 737 airframe had increased by roughly 10% per decade, as passenger volume increased similarly. The decision to halt 757 production in 2005 meant that as far as Boeing was concerned, the 737 was the only game in town for their narrow-body market. The 737's low stance on the ground had served it well for decades. Baggage could be quickly loaded, even without proper belt loaders and ground equipment, and access for maintenance was simple. This benefit slowly became a liability as the decades passed, however. The ability to "stretch" the 737NG, and now the 737 MAX, the newest version, was limited by the landing gear's geometry. The relatively short landing gear would make the aft fuselage prone to contacting the runway during takeoff and landing if the airplane were to be lengthened any further, thus limiting its ultimate capacity.

On the other hand, the 757 could easily be stretched, as evidenced by the advent of the long-body 757-300, because of its larger wing and tall landing gear. Many believe that if the 757 had soldiered on through a few lean years, it would have certainly come into its prime. The long landing gears hold another advantage as well. The newer super-high-bypass engines, which are offering fuel efficiencies improved by more than 30%, tend to be larger in fan diameter than the traditional turbofans that they are replacing today. The 737 MAX design faced challenges with fitting the larger-diameter LEAP-1B engines on its low-stance airframe, but there was ample room under the 757's wings for such improvements. The greater fuel efficiency of these engines would have increased the already long range of the 757 even further too.

Today, with the gift of hindsight, many involved with the 757 program have indicated their belief that discontinuing the 757 was a mistake. Further, the creation of the 757-300 was resisted for years, since, as the reasoning went, the additional passenger capacity of a stretched 757 was too similar to that of the 767. Additionally, due to the low-drag economics of the 757's narrow fuselage, it boasted lower seat-mile costs. This was seen as potentially putting the 757 in direct competition with the 767, a dynamic that was feared by Joe Sutter several years before. There is a distinct possibility that if the 757-300 had been created earlier, sales would have been adequate to weather the lean sales years, and perhaps the program could have persevered.

Opinions and hindsight aside, the 757 proved to be an airplane that was, for its day, incredibly efficient while exhibiting exceptional handling and performance. The dependability of the 757, paired with its exemplary safety record, is certainly noteworthy. Boeing's long-standing philosophy of building airplanes where the pilot is directly in control of the aircraft and completely engaged in its operation certainly played a part in pilot proficiency and thus added to the safety factor. Originally designed to be a domestic aircraft, its routes expanded under the ETOPS rules set forth in the 1980s, becoming a top choice for oceanic flights. In the end, the 757 was an airplane that actually created its own market in many ways. Even today, it's still in widespread passenger service worldwide and is also a popular cargo aircraft, used by big-hitters such as DHL, UPS, and FedEx, effectively replacing the older DC-8 and 727 equipment in operations.

This being said, the 757 story may not necessarily be over. As recently as May 2020, there has been talk of producing a "757-Plus," embracing modern engine and cockpit technology while maintaining low development and production costs. While no formal announcements have yet been made at the time of writing, it certainly seems like a logical way of competing with the Airbus A321neo, while still retaining greater aircraft growth potential and having much longer-range capability. Will this be the end of 757 production? Time will provide the answer.

CHAPTER 7
TECHNICAL DATA

BOEING 757 SYSTEMS OVERVIEW

The Boeing 757 aircraft systems were designed to be robust, redundant, and failure tolerant while also being essentially the same operationally as those on the 767. Having systems common to both increased parts commonality, eased pilot-training requirements, and lent both aircraft to a common design.

ENGINE INDICATION AND CREW-ALERTING SYSTEM (EICAS)

EICAS, which is common to most new jetliners today in one form or another, was first designed for the Boeing 757. This system monitors nearly all aircraft systems and provides the crew status indications by using the cathode ray tubes (CRTs) indigenous to modern EFIS-equipped cockpits. The 757 has two separate EICAS computers, so that if one fails, the other can be selected. If a non-normal condition were to arise, a message

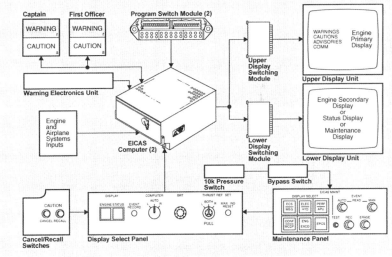

EICAS General Description

Courtesy of the Boeing Company

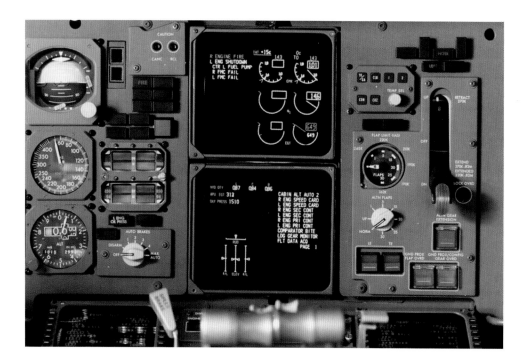

EICAS is designed to monitor aircraft systems and give the crew a prioritized list of malfunctions (*upper left corner of the upper display*). This photo shows what would result in a very busy day in real life. The right engine is showing a red R ENGINE FIRE indication and an exhaust gas temperature (EGT) well in excess of redline, as indicated by the red "649" in the lower right corner of the upper display. *Courtesy of the Boeing Company*

appears on each pilot's upper display unit. These messages fall into three categories:

Warnings (displayed first): A condition that requires rapid corrective action. Cabin depressurization, resulting in a CABIN ALTITUDE indication, would be an example of an EICAS warning.

Cautions (displayed second): A malfunction that requires timely remedial action. A good example of such an alert would be generated by an ENGINE OVERHEAT message, indicating a bleed air leak in the engine nacelle.

Advisories (displayed last): A non-normal situation that is not urgent and requires corrective action only on a time-permitting basis. A failure of a yaw damper system, for example, would generate an advisory to the crew.

EICAS is a central system that communicates with all major aircraft systems and thus "governs" them to a large extent, reducing crew workload. It is also helpful on the ground for aircraft mechanics since it stores faults, allowing for a speedier diagnosis of aircraft system malfunctions. The Status function of the EICAS system can also be used to verify the airplane's dispatch readiness (for more information on EICAS and its development, please see page 40).

ELECTRICAL

ALTERNATING CURRENT (AC) SYSTEM

Electrical power on the 757 is primarily supplied by three 115-volt, 400 Hz generators, with one installed on each engine and the last driven by the auxiliary power unit (APU). Each of these is capable of providing 90 KVA,

Courtesy of the Boeing Company

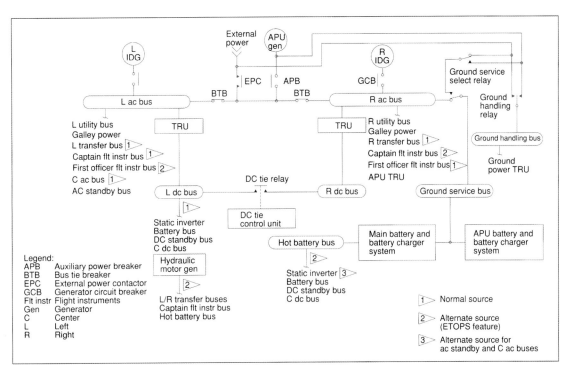

Electrical Power System

allowing any one of these generators to shoulder all of the aircraft's essential electrical loads. In order to provide exactly 400 Hz AC power, each generator must be turning at exactly 6,000 rpm. Since the APU is governed at a constant speed, its accessory drive gears directly turn the generator. The engines must operate at varying speeds, though, from ground idle up to maximum takeoff thrust, so a direct drive for the engine-driven generators is not possible. The engine-mounted generators solve this issue with the use of an integrated drive, similar to an automatic transmission on an automobile.

The electrical system uses a bus power control unit (BPCU) to govern the routing of electrical power to the aircraft's AC busses through the use of electrical switches. Under normal circumstances, the available generator(s) deliver power to the aircraft's 115V AC busses, which in turn are connected to the associated utility busses, galley busses, and onside pilot avionics.

Looking at the schematic, one can see that the 757 electrical system is designed with left- and right-side systems. During normal operation, the left engine's generator powers the left side, while the right engine's generator powers the right side. If an engine generator were to fail, the remaining generator can power the offside busses through the use of bus tie breakers (BTBs). The APU generator can also be used to provide power with the failure of one or both engine generators, or during times when the engines are not operating. When on the ground, AC power can also be provided from external power supplied by the airport.

It is noteworthy that the left and right sides of the electrical system can also be separated in the case of a malfunctioning or shorted bus. In such an extreme emergency, the aircraft is designed to have at least one of each required aircraft system remaining operational through the powered side of the system. In order to increase redundancy, a smaller center AC bus (C AC bus) is provided. The 757 is equipped with a triplex autoland system. For safety during autoland operations, the aircraft employs three separate autopilots that provide a cross-check for one another. Each is powered by a different source, thus requiring the center bus.

DIRECT CURRENT (DC) SYSTEM

While the bulk of the electrical equipment on the 757 is AC powered, there are some devices on the aircraft that must be powered by 28 V direct current (DC). To allow this, the system is equipped with two transformer rectifiers (T/Rs), which convert 115 V AC power to 28 V DC current for these items. This power can also be supplemented by the aircraft's battery.

In the event of a loss of all AC-generating capability, the 757's essential equipment can be powered by the standby busses through the aircraft's battery. The standby DC bus is powered directly from the battery, while the standby AC bus requires an inverter to convert the battery's 28 V DC power

into 115 V AC power. The system is designed to provide enough electrical power to safely perform an emergency landing even if all generating power is lost.

FUEL

The fuel system on the 757 is composed of three tanks. The left and right fuel tanks are located in the wings, between the forward and aft wing spars, mostly outboard of the engines. The center tank is located between the wing spars in the wing carry-through under the cabin floor and inboard wing sections. The left and right tanks have an incorporated dry bay located directly above and behind each engine. This is to prevent punctures to the fuel tank in the event of an uncontained engine failure.

Each tank has two 115 V AC-powered electric boost pumps that ensure positive fuel flow to the engines at all times. To reduce structural loads on the wings, the system

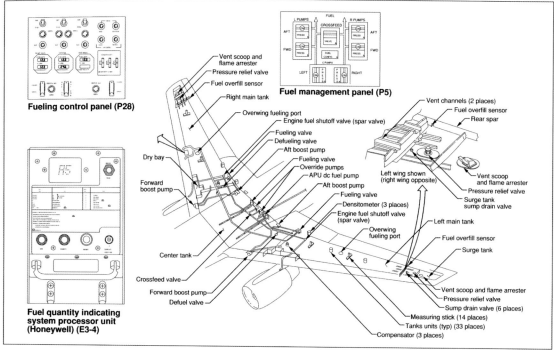

Courtesy of the Boeing Company

Fueling control panel (P28)

Fuel management panel (P5)

Fuel quantity indicating system processor unit (Honeywell) (E3-4)

Vent scoop and flame arrester
Pressure relief valve
Fuel overfill sensor
Right main tank
Overwing fueling port
Engine fuel shutoff valve (spar valve)
Fueling valve
Defueling valve
Aft boost pump
Fueling valve
Override pumps
APU dc fuel pump
Aft boost pump
Fueling valve
Densitometer (3 places)
Engine fuel shutoff valve (spar valve)
Overwing fueling port
Dry bay
Forward boost pump
Center tank
Crossfeed valve
Forward boost pump
Defuel valve

Vent channels (2 places)
Fuel overfill sensor
Rear spar
Left wing shown (right wing opposite)
Vent scoop and flame arrester
Pressure relief valve
Surge tank sump drain valve
Left main tank
Fuel overfill sensor
Surge tank
Vent scoop and flame arrester
Pressure relief valve
Sump drain valve (6 places)
Measuring stick (14 places)
Tanks units (typ) (33 places)
Compensator (3 places)

Fuel System

is designed to use center tank fuel first, if any is required for the flight. When the center tank is empty, under normal operations, each engine begins to feed off its respective wing tank. A motive-flow scavenge pump, powered by the left tank's forward fuel pump, removes any residual fuel left in the center tank and transfers it to the left tank. Two redundant crossfeed valves allow fuel balancing between the left and right tanks, primarily for single-engine operations, allowing the pilot to maintain a balanced fuel load.

Fueling is accomplished using a fueling station located outboard of the right engine on the leading edge of the wing. The desired fuel load can be selected by the fueling technician, and the aircraft will stop fuel flow to each tank when the selected quantity is reached. In case of a malfunction, an overflow system sensor, located in each wing's surge tank, mechanically backs up the automatic system to prevent overfilling. A defueling system is also built into the system to allow defueling back into a truck or hydrant receiver. This system also allows the transfer of fuel from one tank to another while the aircraft is on the ground. To allow further operational flexibility, a gravity-fueling port is located on the top of each wing to make the 757 compatible with differing airport equipment.

HYDRAULICS

The 757 employs three separate hydraulic systems to provide redundancy to enable the aircraft to be malfunction tolerant while maintaining a safe level of functionality and control. Hydraulic pressure of 3,000 psi is provided by the left, center, and right hydraulic systems. Primary flight controls (aileron, elevator, and rudder) and autopilot servos can be powered in a triple-redundant fashion by any of the three systems. Other systems, such as the elevator feel unit, stabilizer trim, yaw dampers, and wheel brakes, can be powered by two of the three systems. Landing gear retraction and steering, along with flaps and slats, are primarily powered only by the left

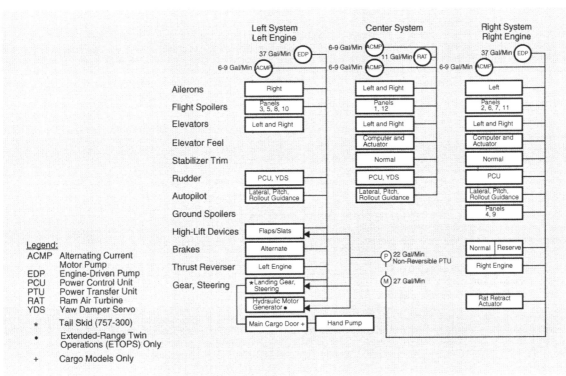

Courtesy of the Boeing Company

Hydraulic Power Distribution

system but are given redundancy by a power transfer unit (PTU), which uses right-system pressure to turn a pump. This pump uses residual left-system fluid to operate these items in the event that the left-system engine-driven pump (EDP) is compromised. For ETOPS operation, a hydraulically driven generator provides electrical redundancy, which can be powered by either the left system or the right system through the PTU. The thrust reversers (left and right) are directly powered from their respective hydraulic system.

The left and right hydraulic systems are each powered by an EDP and an AC-powered electric motor pump (ACMP). The center system is powered by two separately-powered ACMPs. Since the aircraft must still be controllable in the event of a failure of both engines and a loss of normal electric power, the 757 is equipped with a ram air turbine (RAT). The RAT is located in the right-side aft wing-to-body fairing and, when deployed, can provide enough limited hydraulic power to the center system for adequate aircraft control. Automatic RAT deployment requires no pilot action and occurs when there is a failure of both engines (rotation less than idle), when the aircraft is airborne, and at an airspeed greater than 80 knots.

AIR SYSTEMS

PNEUMATICS

The 757, like most jetliners, uses engine bleed air as the primary means of providing air-conditioning and pressurization. Jet engines function by compressing air for fuel combustion, which in turn provides the thrust for flight. High-pressure bleed air is extracted from the engines' compressors by use of bleed air valves, which control the pressure and, if necessary, can also shut off the flow. Pressurized air can also be provided, both in flight and on the ground, by the aircraft's auxiliary power unit (APU) for air-conditioning and the engines' pneumatic starters. While at the gate, this pressurized air can also be provided by an air cart (sometimes referred to as a "huffer cart"), through hookups located in

the forward portion of the wing-to-body fairing. In addition to air-conditioning/pressurization and engine starting, compressed air is also used for pressurizing the hydraulic reservoir and potable water tank, as well as providing thermal anti-icing for the wing and engines. In order to make the system redundant, the pneumatic manifold incorporates an isolation valve, which can separate the two sides in the event of a leak or malfunction.

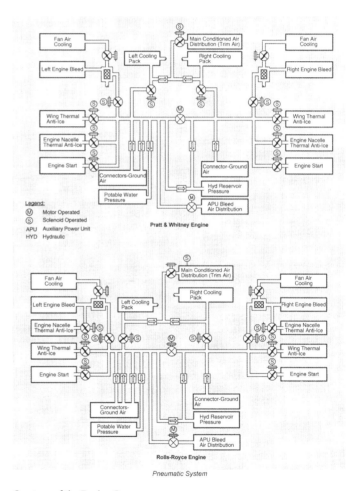

Courtesy of the Boeing Company

AIR-CONDITIONING

The 757 uses two air cycle machines, more commonly known as "packs," to provide air-conditioning. The left pack is operated by the left side of the pneumatic system, while the right pack is provided pressure from the right side of the manifold. Recall that because of the rapid compression of the bleed air in the engines' compressors, the air arriving at the pack valve is at a very high temperature. A small amount of this air is bypassed, to be reintroduced later to provide temperature control. The rest of the hot air is sent to the primary heat exchanger, which cools it before being sent to the compressor, where both its temperature and pressure are increased. From the compressor, the hot, high-pressure air is sent through a secondary heat exchanger to cool it. From there, it is sent to a turbine that drives the compressor via a mechanical shaft. As the air passes through the turbine, its pressure is reduced, making it quite cold before it goes into the mix manifold. Some of the bypassed hot air is then reintroduced into the system to provide automatic temperature control on a zone-by-zone basis. The 757-200 uses a three-zone system, while the longer 757-300 uses four separate zones by drawing cold air from the two packs.

Courtesy of the Boeing Company

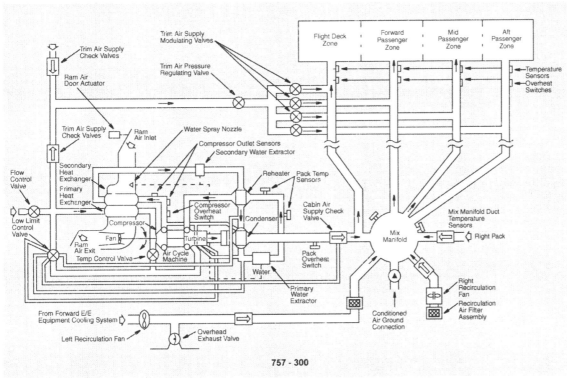

757 - 300

Conditioned Air Supply

CABIN PRESSURIZATION

Like all modern jetliners, the 757 relies on a pressurized cabin to provide breathable cabin pressures while operating at high altitudes. The source of this pressurized air is from the air-conditioning packs, whose temperature-controlled output is forced into the cabin through numerous vents via the mix manifold. Precise cabin pressure is maintained by the outflow valve, located on the lower left side of the aft fuselage. The valve is electrically moved to a more open position to decrease cabin pressure, or to a more closed position to increase cabin pressure. A dual, redundant automatic controller is used to control the valve. Each channel is powered by a separate electrical source and controls two separate motors on the outflow valve. In the cockpit, prior to departure,

the pilot needs only to set the landing-field elevation, desired mode, and maximum limit for cabin pressure change. The rest is automatic, substantially reducing pilot workload.

FLIGHT CONTROLS

The 757 flight control system is quite conventional. Each of the primary flight control functions (roll, pitch, and yaw) are provided with triple-redundant power, utilizing the left, center, and right hydraulic systems.

Roll (banking side to side) control is accomplished by the use of ailerons working in opposition, assisted by flight spoilers. If the pilot wishes to enter a left bank, the yoke is turned to the left. This causes the aileron on the left wing

Courtesy of the Boeing Company

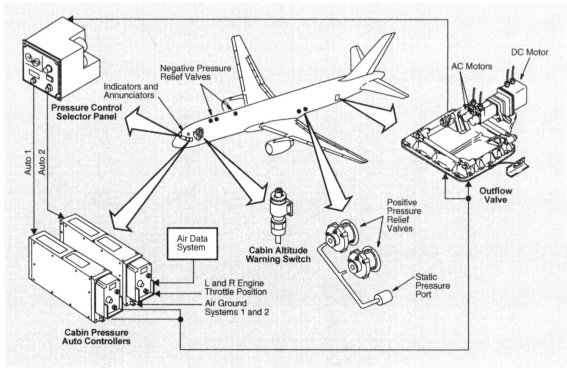

Cabin Pressurization System

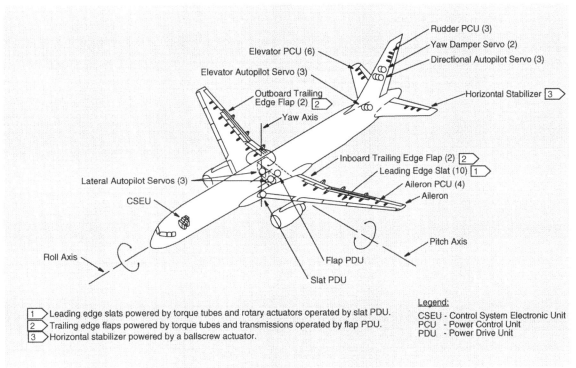

Flight Control Actuators, Servos, and Electronics

to rise, while its counterpart on the right wing is lowered. This creates an imbalance of lift, causing the aircraft to roll into a left bank. The aileron action is assisted by the flight spoilers, which rise only on the wing that is being lowered to enhance roll authority.

Pitch (nose up and down) control is accomplished by the use of elevators mounted on the trailing edges of the horizontal stabilizers. If the pilot pulls aft on the yoke, this raises both elevators, which aerodynamically forces the tail down, thus raising the nose. The opposite is true when the yoke is pushed forward, causing the aircraft's nose to drop. Due to the wide loading range of the 757, combined with its large speed range, the 757 is equipped with a variable-incidence horizontal stabilizer to provide speed trimming for pitch stabilization.

Yaw (nose side to side) control is accomplished by the rudder, located in the trailing edge of the vertical stabilizer. This surface is controlled by the rudder pedals located in front of each pilot. Pushing on the left rudder pedal displaces the rudder surface to the left. This aerodynamically forces the tail to the right and swings the nose to the left. Naturally, pressing the right pedal causes the opposite reaction and swings the nose to the right. The rudder is primarily used for single-engine operations where thrust from the wing-mounted engines is asymmetric, and during takeoff and landing with crosswinds. A secondary (but important) function of the rudder is to reduce Dutch roll, an alternating rolling and yawing motion characteristic of swept-wing jets. Dual-redundant yaw dampers automatically provide small rudder inputs to null this undesirable effect.

The secondary flight controls on the 757 consist of the high-lift devices that enable the 757 to operate at low takeoff and approach speeds when extended, while allowing it to be quite swift in cruise flight when retracted. In preparation for takeoff or landing, the trailing edge flaps are extended. When this occurs, the leading edge slats also deploy. The combination of the leading edge slats and trailing edge flaps causes the curvature (or camber) of the top of the wing to be greatly increased, along with the effective wing area to some extent. The increase in camber improves lift significantly at low speeds.

SYSTEMS CONCLUSION

While this description of 757 systems is more topical by nature, one can get a general idea of how the aircraft's systems function. Moreover, it becomes apparent that a great amount of redundancy was built into the aircraft to ensure its safety even if multiple failures were to occur. Indeed, the splitting of the electrical and hydraulic systems into separate left, right, and center systems is a good example of the elegant solutions Boeing found to build safety into the 757's design.

Boeing 757 Specifications

	757-200	757-300
Length	155' 3"	178' 7"
Wingspan	124" 10"	124' 10"
Wingspan With Winglets	134' 7"	134' 7"
Height	44' 6"	44' 6"
Max Takeoff Weight (Pounds)	220,000 (Basic) 230,000* 240,000* 255,000*	240,000 (Basic) 273,000*
Max Landing Weight (Pounds)	198,000 210,000*	224,000
Max Standard Fuel Capacity (US Gallons)	11,489	11,466
Powerplant (Thrust in Pounds)	RB.211-535C (37,400)** RB.211-535E4 (40,100)** RB.211-535E4B (43,100)** PW2037 (38,200)** PW2040 (41,700)**	RB.211-E4B (43,100)** PW2043 (43,850)**
Vmo (Knots)/Mmo	350/M.86	350/M.86
Range-Full Fuel (nm)	3,910 (PW2040)	3,395 (PW2043)
Service Ceiling (Feet)	42,000	42,000
Seating Capacity (FAA Limit)	221 (Overwing Exit Configuration) 228 (Four Door Configuration)	280
Standard Baggage Compartment Capacity (Cubic Feet)	1,670	2,370

*Optional
**Based on Boeing data- FAA TCDS information differs slightly based on conditions

Courtesy of the Boeing Company

COCKPIT PANELS

PILOTS' MAIN PANEL

Courtesy of the Boeing Company via Duane Jackson

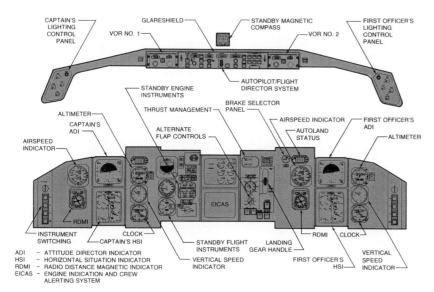

ADI – ATTITUDE DIRECTOR INDICATOR
HSI – HORIZONTAL SITUATION INDICATOR
RDMI – RADIO DISTANCE MAGNETIC INDICATOR
EICAS – ENGINE INDICATION AND CREW
ALERTING SYSTEM

PILOTS' OVERHEAD PANEL

Courtesy of the Boeing Company via Duane Jackson

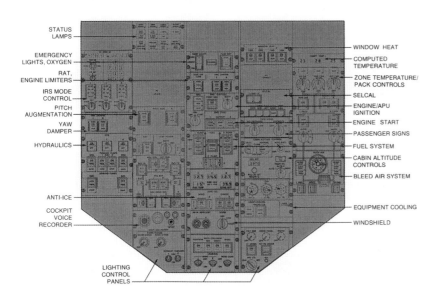

CONTROL STAND AND MAINTENANCE PANEL

Courtesy of the Boeing Company via Duane Jackson

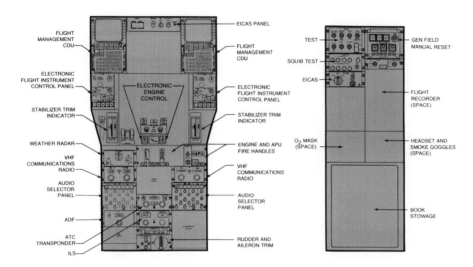

757 WALK-AROUND

A pilot's preflight walk-around inspection normally begins in the cockpit. The aircraft being inspected today is a United Parcel Service Boeing 757-200PF. A check of the aircraft's metal-covered maintenance log, commonly known as "the can," ensures that the aircraft is safe to operate and fly. After bringing up electrical power and ensuring that proper documentation is on board, the pilot (normally the first officer) begins to inspect the outside of the aircraft.

On the nose of the aircraft, beneath the first officer's side window, are the right and aux pitot tubes (seen here covered with red "REMOVE BEFORE FLIGHT" flags) and the angle of attack probe. The black cord behind the nose landing gear strut supplies 115 V 400-cycle AC power to the airplane via the ground power receptacle. The probe located just forward of and below the word "commerce" is the total air temperature probe, which supplies information to the aircraft's air data computers. Just aft and below this

are the two flush, silver-colored static ports. Note the lack of galley and passenger boarding doors, a trait common to the PF version of the 757.

Courtesy of Airlinercafe.com via Ahmed R. Orgunwall

After the pilot has come down the airstair, the inspection begins at the nose landing gear. The condition of the tires and the extension of the shock strut are common focus areas. The shiny metal bar between the two tires is the attach point for the tow bar and pushback tug.

Courtesy of Airlinercafe.com via Ahmed R. Orgunwall

Moving aft along the lower fuselage, the condition of the right distance-measuring equipment (DME) antenna (*front*), approach marker beacon (*middle*), and right VHF communications antenna (*aft*) is assessed. From this vantage point, the general condition of the right engine can be observed, noting any fluid leaks or damage.

Courtesy of Airlinercafe.com via Ahmed R. Orgunwall

A closer view of the right engine shows the detail of the engine inlet. Minor foreign-object damage to blades (*green arrow*), within specific limits, is permissible provided that the damage is dressed (filed down) and thoroughly inspected. The fan shrouding has a rubbing strip (*blue arrow*) that keeps a tight seal to the fan blade tips but is soft enough that if some rubbing occurs, the blades are not damaged. Some wear, such as shown here, is normal and not cause for concern. The perforated inlet skin (*orange arrow*) reduces the engine's noise signature.

Courtesy of Airlinercafe.com via Ahmed R. Orgunwall

Looking at the engine from the rear allows for an inspection of the thrust reverser components and blocker doors inside the fan cowl. Equally important is the condition of the turbine blades in the exhaust, since a missing turbine blade or stator vane would be cause for concern.

Courtesy of Airlinercafe.com via Ahmed R. Orgunwall

A closer look forward through the fan duct gives a better view of the thrust reverser blocker doors (*green arrows*), shown here in the forward thrust position. When thrust reverse is selected, these doors move into position to block the fan air from exiting out the back of the cowl. Instead, it is deflected forward through an exposed opening in the cowling, helping to slow the aircraft after landing or during a rejected takeoff.

Courtesy of Airlinercafe.com via Ahmed R. Orgunwall

Looking forward from underneath the right wing, the two variable-geometry pack heat-exchanger exhausts can be seen under the wing-to-body fairings. A drain mast is also visible on the forward part of the fairing.

Courtesy of Airlinercafe.com via Ahmed R. Orgunwall

The right main landing gear is inspected for signs of tire wear and fluid leaks from brake lines and the shock strut. If the aircraft has recently flown, the pilot is also on the lookout for smoking brakes, since this can be indicative of a fluid leak into the brake assembly or overheated brake components, which would need to be assessed by maintenance personnel.

While inspecting the undersides of the wings, ensuring that there are no fuel leaks is critically important. Each of the oval-shaped panels allows maintenance access to the associated fuel tank, and, if the normal fuel quantity indicator fails, indexed measuring sticks (*green arrow*) use a magnetic float to give an indication as to how much fuel is in the tank. The stick is turned a quarter of a turn, allowing it to drop down from the bottom of the wing until the physical level of the fuel inside the tank is reached. The index number can be read from the stick where it exits the wing skin. This number is then compared to a chart to determine the exact quantity on board.

Courtesy of Airlinercafe.com via Ahmed R. Orgunwall

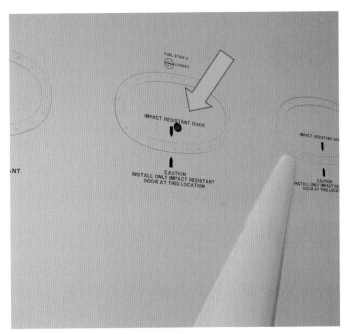

Courtesy of Airlinercafe.com via Ahmed R. Orgunwall

Courtesy of Airlinercafe.com via Ahmed R. Orgunwall

The ram air turbine (RAT) is located in the right aft wing-to-body fairing on the 757. This device will deploy from this location if the need for emergency hydraulic power for the aircraft's flight controls is required.

Courtesy of Airlinercafe.com via Ahmed R. Orgunwall

Stepping back from the aircraft a bit gives the pilot an eagle's-eye view of the machine. Note that when hydraulic power is removed from the aircraft, the elevators tend to droop, which is normal while the airplane is parked.

Courtesy of Airlinercafe.com via Ahmed R. Orgunwall

This is a view from ground level looking up at the auxiliary power unit (APU) with the servicing doors open. This unit, an AiResearch GTCP 331-200, is a small jet engine that can supply electrical power and bleed air to the aircraft either when the engines are not operating or in flight during a non-normal condition.

Courtesy of the Boeing Company

This vantage offers a great view of the variable-incidence horizontal stabilizer. Below and forward of the stabilizer, outlined with a red box, is the pressurization outflow valve. Normally it is seen in the full-open position while on the ground.

Moving forward along the left side of the aft fuselage, we find the static air pressure ports for the pressurization and elevator control feel systems. Both of these systems, along with the aircraft's air data computers, require a measurement of outside air pressure to carry out their functions properly.

A view of the left wingtip shows the forward-mounted red and aft-mounted white navigation lights. Six static wicks are shown here. As their name implies, they are installed to dissipate static electricity and improve radio reception, particularly during flight through precipitation. The clear lens, located at mid-wingtip, is for the anticollision strobe light. The strobe light is not usually used on the ground because it is extremely bright and can distract the pilots of other nearby aircraft. The blue arrow indicates the position of the NACA-type fuel tank vent.

After walking around the left wing, which is essentially a mirror image of the right, we get to the forward wing-to-body fairing. The open scoop allows air to enter the left air-conditioning pack heat exchangers. This door, as indicated by the placard, is a variable-geometry scoop that articulates dependent on the cooling needs of the pack.

Courtesy of Airlinercafe.com via Ahmed R. Orgunwall

Moving forward along the left-side forward fuselage, we can inspect the most prominent feature of the 757-200PF, the large main-deck cargo door. The condition of the latches is of primary importance because they will bear all of the door's pressurization loads while the aircraft is in flight.

Courtesy of Airlinercafe.com via Ahmed R. Orgunwall

Back where we started, at the nose of the airplane. Satisfied that the aircraft is ready for flight, the first officer will generally return to the cockpit to complete the required equipment tests and set up the cockpit for flight. This view shows the pilot's entry door, which is much smaller than the standard L1 door on a passenger-carrying 757.

Courtesy of Airlinercafe.com via Ahmed R. Orgunwall

FLYING THE 757 WITH GLEN MARSHALL

For fourteen years, I flew the Boeing 757-200-series aircraft, powered by Rolls-Royce RB211-535E4 engines, for a major airline. What an amazing machine! It is the Super Cub of the airline world, and I cannot say enough good things about it. Most pilots who have flown it feel the same as I do. I enjoyed manually flying it as much as possible, because it handles very well. The level of automation, I think, was exactly right. It can do everything, including land itself down to exceptionally low visibility, but you can still turn the automation off and just hand-fly it too. Its performance is legendary, and it will do things that no other airliner can do.

I had wanted to fly one since I was a little kid, and I remember when the 757 and 767 were first being designed,

Courtesy of the Boeing Company

and my father showing me pictures of what they would look like. I just thought the 757 looked cool even then. A long while later, when I was in college, I had the opportunity to be an intern at a major airline that flew 757s. Back then, long before 9/11, as an intern I could ride in a cockpit jump seat in any of the aircraft my airline flew, and I did so as often as I could. The 757 was always the most fun.

Years later, I became an airline pilot myself. As a new hire, I was assigned to fly the 737s, both -200s and -300s, but always wanted to fly the 757. My airline paid pilots the same rate to fly all the different fleet types, and the most-senior pilots generally chose to fly the 757 because they loved flying it. After about four years flying the 737, I was finally senior enough to be one of those flying it.

In ground school, I was amazed by the systems. It was like they took a 737 and just developed the thought further in each case. The systems pretty much take care of themselves, and you can just focus on stick-and-rudder flying, like in a Piper Cub. On startup, generators come online by themselves and power transfers as needed, all without action from the pilots. From a pilot's point of view, it is much simpler than the 737s that I was coming from. We looked at the performance numbers, and I could not believe what the numbers said. It got to the point in ground school that checking the performance was kind of a joke, since it could mostly always do whatever you asked of it. The ground school instructor bet us that we would never have to do a full-power takeoff for performance reasons.

The first flight I did at the controls of a 757 was from Phoenix to Las Vegas, and from there on to New York's JFK airport. In Phoenix and Las Vegas, I was very proud that now I was finally flying the BIG airplane. In a sea of 737s and A320s, we were the big fish. However, when we landed at JFK, I was immediately humbled by once again being one of the small airplanes. I learned quickly that there is always someone flying something bigger or faster than what you are! Later, taking off out of JFK, I was just grinning from ear to ear as the airplane just pointed at the sky. That began my fourteen-year love affair with the 757.

In the simulator, we had practiced engine failures at all points of the flight; when an engine quits on final approach, we could retract the flaps partway like you have do to in most airplanes, but the amazing thing was, you didn't have to. The go-around performance on one engine was good enough to just press on. My airline flew some of the oldest and highest-time 757s in the world. We had some that were purchased from Eastern Airlines, some from Republic Airlines, and a few that we had built new just for us. They were all a little different and had a range of gross weights, from 230,000 pounds up to 255,000 pounds. Some of the 737-200s and most of the 737-300s that I had flown, even though the 737 is a much-older model than the 757s, were newer than our 757s. Near the end of my time flying the airplane, we obtained some newer ones from ATA Airlines, US Airways, and also from North American, a charter company.

Flying the 757 domestically, the performance was fascinating. Our airplanes all had "round dials," and just a little of the early glass-cockpit technology. On initial climb-out, domestically, it was normal to climb at a rate of more than 6,000 feet per minute. I do not know what the number was, because the gauge went up only to 6,000, up or down. We would rotate and lift off, and the needle would almost immediately bury itself at the top of the scale. The speed brakes were amazingly effective, and you could descend at those rates too. Normally we would use reduced power for takeoff and climb to make the engines last longer.

On flights from Orange County to Phoenix or Las Vegas, we would always use full power, which was a real treat. It was such a short flight that we did not have to carry as much fuel, so the airplane was light. Because of the noise restrictions out of Orange County, we would do a maximum-performance takeoff and then sort of coast over the top to be high and quiet over the noise monitor. We would set the brakes and run up the power, and the whole airplane would quiver with excitement. Then we would release the brakes and just hold on for dear life. In just a few seconds, we were at flying speed and then just pointed the nose at the sky and went. It was really a thrill to do, but everything happened faster than normal, and you really had to be paying attention to do the procedure correctly.

757s excel at flying all over North America and in the mountainous regions of South America because of their range and performance. My airline started to fly them to the Hawaiian Islands from the western states, and for thirteen of my fourteen years on the airplane I flew it mostly back and forth to Hawaii, and occasionally to Cancun, Mexico. I cannot think of a better airplane for flying to Hawaii. On those flights, we got to use them to their full potential and frequently took off close to our maximum takeoff weight on hot days in the summer. Even under those conditions, we still were able to do reduced-power takeoffs. Occasionally we did need full power. Even at those heavy weights, we could always initially climb to at least 35,000 feet, and much of the time straight to 37,000 feet. Some of the runways in Hawaii are short, by airliner standards, such as those at Maui and Lihue. The 757s never had any problem with them. Some other airlines, flying other airplane types, would have to offload some of their passengers, bags, or cargo in order to make the takeoff safely, and then put all that weight on our flights, because we could still carry it. Landing on short, wet runways was fun in the 757 because it had a slow approach speed due to its excellent wing design and had equally excellent brakes. In fourteen years of flying it, I never once had a brake-cooling issue after landing, which can be a problem in other aircraft. The flight controls were very responsive but felt relatively heavy compared to other modern airliners, and in the ever-present gusty crosswinds in Hawaii, they worked very well. We got a lot of practice with crosswind takeoff and landing in Hawaii.

The cockpit floor is lower than the main cabin floor. When we worked with flight attendants who were new to the airplane, we always had to remind them that talking to 757 pilots was a "step down." Some forgot and did stumble down the step into the cockpit. When I was assigned to ferry empty airplanes, if we had flight attendants with us, they were always amazed by the climb rates. I also had the opportunity to pick up a few of our airplanes out of a heavy-maintenance facility and fly them back to our airline's main base. Those trips were always remarkably interesting because we would do a test flight first. We had a "task card" that we had to accomplish for these maintenance flights, and it included a very thorough preflight inspection that took several hours, followed by a local flight that took about an hour and a half to complete. The flight included checking all the systems, flipping the "dusty switches" that do not get used in a normal flight. That even included deploying and testing the ram air turbine (RAT), which provides hydraulic power to run the flight controls if both engines fail. The RAT looks like a small outboard motor that, when deployed, pops out of the belly of the airplane on the right side, behind the wing. To test the RAT, we had to turn off the normal hydraulic pumps for one of the systems and then manually deploy it. Nearly immediately, it spun up and supplied the hydraulic pressure on that system (the other two were still always powered) right at 3000 psi, where it should be. That inspired confidence in me that even the backup systems worked well.

I am incredibly grateful that I got to fly 757s as long as I did. They are exceptionally reliable and fun to fly. They look like a bird of prey coming in for landing. Their performance reputation is well earned, and worldwide they have proved to be one of the safest airplanes ever built. Flying an empty 757, with its awesome performance, does not make money for the airline, but it does make the pilots giggle.

THE AUTHOR
DAN DORNSEIF

Dan Dornseif has been directly involved with aviation for over three decades, holds FAA type ratings on the Boeing 737 and Embraer Brasilia, and is currently a captain and check airman for a major airline in the United States. When he is not flying jetliners, Dan enjoys spending time with family, flying antique aircraft, and building model airplanes.